Steps of an

Everyday Christian

Nora Peacock

The
Father's
Quill

Steps of an Everyday Christian

Published by The Father's Quill

Copyright © 2013 Nora Peacock

ISBN 978-0615828336

Poem *Time Passing* by Leota Littleton
All other poetry by Nora Peacock
Logo design by Andrew Lavier
Author's photo by Hayes Peterson

www.thefathersquill.com

Dedication

To Marcia Mitchell aka Marcie Nootenboom
How can I thank you for the selfless gift
of your time to mentor me?
When life's struggles added up to years
without the completion of this book,
memories of your encouraging words
made the difference.

Thank you, dear friend.

My deepest appreciation to Phyllis Gates
for the many hours of labor
in creating the touching pictures for
Steps of an Everyday Christian

My gratitude goes beyond measure
to my resident techie, Arlen,
who devoted countless hours to
helping his computer-challenged wife.
Your infinite patience knows no bounds.
What a precious gift you are to me.

Thank You, dear reader, for hanging out
with this *Everyday Christian.*

Above all, thank you Lord Jesus,
for holding me by the hand
through every step of my life's journey.
Without You, I could do nothing.

*"Righteousness will go before Him
and shall make His footsteps our pathway."
Psalm 85:13*

Introduction

Luke 12:48 tells me, *"... For everyone to whom much is given, from him much will be required ..."* Several years ago, my husband, Arlen, and I enjoyed living in a 3200 square foot house on three acres in the country. I seldom had a problem with our *ya'll come* policy until our pastor asked if we would house an evangelist and his family for several weeks.

My answer? "No way!"

A Christian most of my life, one would think I'd not wear my insecurities on my sleeve. But I had put the evangelist, Jerry, on a pedestal. What's more, I felt convinced this man of God would see my every fault and shake his finger at me in stern correction. I also knew that confessing my fears would sadden him. Jerry focused not on my failings, but on glorifying the Savior he loved and served.

Fortunately, I saw the error of my ways in time to go back to my pastor and say yes. In the process of wrestling with my fears, I gave myself a far sterner talking-to than Jerry would have ever thought about doing. I soon recognized that this man had to get up and brush his teeth, comb his hair, and put his shoes on—just like me. Although his effectiveness in doing God's work was great, he lived the life of an *Everyday Christian* who put one foot in front of the other. He could have decided that any number of personal issues would disqualify him from serving Christ. But, he chose not to go there. And eventually—so did I.

The seed for this book came from that experience of almost missing out on the blessings God had in store for me and for my family. I had to make a decision. Would I put on my shoes and walk out my faith by trusting God to guide my steps—even though I might falter—or would I grab my shoes and then run from opportunities for service in which I could bless others?

Steps of an Everyday Christian speaks of everyday people, with everyday weaknesses and strengths, living everyday life. I share stories from a less-than-perfect memory, while holding true to the lessons God continues teaching His daughter-in-process. Any errors are mine. I pray that you will find the freedom and joy that Jesus gives as He works through each of us, despite all that comes with our human frailties.

Your fellow traveler,

Nora

Table of Contents

All Things New

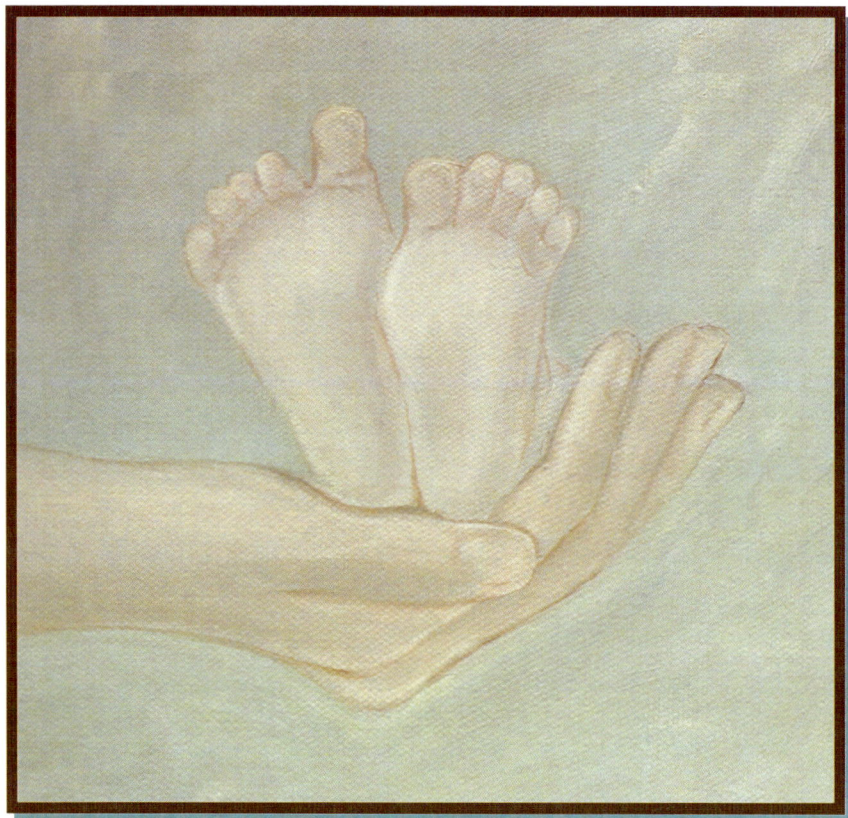

Steps

A New Point of View

Recycled Riches

Wakeup Time

Mama on the Move

Cromensators

Make Believe

New in the News

User Friendly

Drawing a Blank

Hot Chocolate

His Princess

Time Passing
Poem

*"Therefore, if anyone is in Christ, he is a new creation,
old things have passed away;
behold, all things have become new."
2 Corinthians 5:17*

A New Point of View

Scripture Trail: Psalm19:1, Psalm 24:1, Isaiah 55:12-13

Stepping Stone: Psalm 19:1

> *"The heavens declare the glory of God; and the firmament shows His handiwork."*

Grandma Grace lived all her life in Wichita, Kansas. I grew up near Portland, Oregon. The geography of these two spots on the map stands worlds apart—more like planets apart.

Kansas is spelled *F-L-A-T*. Driving over a hill constitutes an outing. Kansans call these occasional mounds of dirt 'mountains.' They obviously haven't seen Oregon's magnificent peaks. Majestic Mount Hood rises 11,239 feet in elevation. Many Oregonians and Washingtonians build their homes on lots that offer spectacular views all along the Cascade Range.

When I visited Kansas, I stared at endless stretches of nothingness. Grandma Grace reveled in the freedom of 360 degrees of wide-open spaces. Her eyes sparkled as she declared, "In Kansas you can see for miles!" I thought, *miles of what?* Grandma beheld beauty in the vast treeless plains. Gazing at the distant horizon, the word 'barren' didn't enter her thinking.

Then there's *Ory-gun*. I see beauty and splendor with every snow-capped vista. But for Grandma Grace, our towering mountains gave her spells of claustrophobia. I can still hear her complaining, "You can't see over the next hill." *She never did get her hills and mountains straight.*

When we meet in heaven, I expect to hear Grandma exclaim, "Honey, you can see forever!" While she extols the infinite expanses of heaven, I will look for lofty mountain's grandeur. Truth is, I believe we will all stand amazed when our heavenly eyes discover the hidden and startling beauty that others now behold on earth.

Prayer Pathway: *Thank You Lord, that You create beauty as unique as the people You love.*

Recycled Riches

Scripture Trail: Isaiah 1:18, Matthew 13:44-46, 2 Corinthians 5:17

Stepping Stone: 2 Corinthians 5:17

> *"Therefore, if anyone is in Christ, he is a new creation; old things are passed away; behold, all things have become new."*

"One person's junk is another chump's treasure." Ask any driver whose car sports an 'I Brake for Yard Sales' bumper sticker. Chances are her backseat holds at least a few *gotta have* items purchased in someone's driveway. The proud owner boasts of walking away with a *steal of a deal.* As a veteran at hosting yard sales, I learned a long time ago to not expect top dollar for my junk. That's okay. What goes around comes around.

Cheap prices on nice items at yard sales and garage sales no longer surprise me. What does blow me away is seeing the stuff for which people willingly part with their hard-earned money. How about Aunt Matilda's rusted bird cage—minus the perch? Some clever shopper looks past the sorry excuse for a bird's home and sees the ugly rusted wires spray painted in gold. Give the crafty lady a few hours and she'll add sprigs of silk flowers and ivy to her 'new' planter.

There was a time that the sale-driven wife spent her evenings convincing her husband that his paycheck had been well-spent. Things have changed. Nowadays, the man of the house walks through the front door with a sheepish look on his face. His beloved bride takes one look at his guilty mug and nails him before he can say, "But honey …"

Hands on hips, the missus asks, "What computer thingamajig did you buy *this time*?

How astounding that God looks past my junk and sees riches!

Prayer Pathway: *God, I ask You to recycle the old me until the new me reflects the riches of Your glory.*

Wakeup Time

Scripture Trail: Psalm 51:9-10, Psalm 118:24, Ezekiel 18:31

Stepping Stone: Psalm 118:24

> *"This is the day the LORD has made; we will rejoice and be glad in it."*

Let's face it. There are days when life stinks. I wake up with a hitch in my get-along, stub my toe on the bedpost, and then limp to the kitchen.

A fresh-brewed cup of my favorite java will fix what ails me. With half-opened eyes I grab a paper filter, fill up the water reservoir, add fresh-ground hazelnut coffee, and hit the ON button. The heavenly scent soon wafts its way through my lethargy.

Time for a bowl of cereal. I stumble to the fridge and pull out a jug of milk ... an all-but-empty jug. *Somebody's head is gonna roll.*

While I ponder my milk crisis, from the corner of my eye, I notice brown water trickling down my white cabinets. Yikes! The coffee pot has backed up. I dash over and hit the OFF button and grab a wad of paper towels. I've been up for what ... eight minutes?

Cleanup time for this old girl. With one hand on my aching back, I wipe wet coffee grounds off the cabinets and floor. I spend another five minutes sopping up java juice, speckled with a bazillion coffee grounds that have found their beady little way into every crevice on my tiled countertop. Out goes the frayed filter and globby mess. I'm gonna have my wakeup cup or else.

Or else what?

What indeed. An empty milk jug morphs into a major meltdown? *Get real.* Maybe it's time I smell the coffee and get with the program.

Prayer Pathway: *Father, this is a new day. Don't let me spoil it.*

Mama on the Move

Scripture Trail: Ruth 1:16, Proverbs 31:26-28, Isaiah 43:19

Stepping Stone: Proverbs 31:28

"Her children rise up and call her blessed ..."

Thirty-six years of living in one location. How does a person lock the door and walk away from a house whose walls have contained the greatest of joys and the deepest of sorrows?

After graduating from high school at 18, my mother-in-law enjoyed 67 years of independence. Then she moved in with me and Arlen—her little boy of 61 years. Mom's daughter, Beth, and her granddaughter, Rhonda, spent weeks sorting her belongings and precious keepsakes.

In the midst of heart-wrenching change, this special woman said goodbyes to dear friends, and a beloved church family. With all the anxiety that comes with drastic change, Mom faced the future with courage, grace, and humor.

Preparing to combine households, Mom, Arlen, and I searched for just the right place to meet our needs. As we looked at one house after another, we could almost read each other's thoughts. "Yep, this one looks pretty nice, but too many stairs. That steep driveway won't work. The gargoyle planter must go. No, we can't ask the owner if we can redo her freshly-painted orange and green rooms..."

Mom embraced a new home with us, creating treasured memories of shared laughter and tears. After three years living at our house, she spent the last four years of her life with Beth and her husband, Gordon. Mom has now made one last grand move to the mansion Jesus prepared just for her.

Mother. Grandmother. Great grandmother. We indeed remember and call her *blessed.*

Prayer Pathway: *May I take time to speak blessing over stand-in parents and parents-in-fact.*

Cromensators (kraw men sá tōrz)

Scripture Trail: Romans 12:4, 1 Corinthians 12:12-22, 1 Peter 4:10

Stepping Stone: 1 Corinthians 12:21

> *"...the eye cannot say to the hand, 'I have no need of you'; nor again the head to the feet, 'I have no need of you.'"*

Somebody out there makes whatchamacallits, thingamabobs, and widgets. There is now an inclusive term for these essential products which one can find in *The Peacock Unabridged Dictionary of Oddball Words*.

And what might that be one might ask ... *and then again—maybe not.*

Nevertheless, here it is: *Cromensator.* My husband's brilliant friend, Don, invented this clever word 50 years ago. It's stood the test of time in our household as a catchall word for anything we can't quite wrap words around. Even more remarkable than this ingenious linguistic marvel is the list of gizmos that fall under the aforementioned umbrella.

Once in a while, a cromensator's true hidden identity gets revealed. One such doohickey—a CD Stomper—came to my attention several years ago. I'd noticed its presence a few times on a table and thought, *What on earth?* Maybe if Google had been available, I could've found the answer somewhere in cyberspace.

Somebody out there makes the doodads (another subgroup of cromensators) that cut elbow macaroni into a gazillion little pieces. Macaroni and cheese lovers of the world (i.e. every kid in America under age 10) owe a profound debt of gratitude to this mechanical marvel. And the incredible people who make the widgets on top of spray cans? How would a woman ever make her hair stay put without them?

To all the widget, thingamabob, doodad, whatchamacallit, and doohickey makers of the world, my sincere kudos. Where would I be without you?

Prayer Pathway: *Father, thank You that in Your divine plan, You created us to need one another.*

Make Believe

Scripture Trail: Habakkuk 1:5, Mark 9:23, John 6:28-29

Stepping Stone: John 6:29

> *"Jesus answered and said, 'This is the work of God, that you believe in Him whom He sent.'"*

Children love to play *Make Believe*. So do grownups.

Parenting a large brood of kids meant witnessing lots of thrills and spills. Battered and scarred household furniture came with the territory. During my childrearing years, I occasionally approached my ever-so-patient husband, Arlen, with ridiculous questions like: "Wouldn't it be nice to have a glass-top coffee table, dear? How about an off-white carpet to brighten up the living room?" He'd give me a cross-eyed *get-real-woman* look as though recalling a child's peanut butter and jelly sandwich landing face down on our ever-so-practical brown-mottled carpet.

My *House Beautiful* daydreams lived in glossy-paged magazines, forever just out of reach. By the time our last child grew up, the grandchildren proved timeless truths: *Beautiful carpets beg for touches of red juice and glass-topped tables make great surfaces for racing cars.* Our grandson, Caleb, paints exquisite food art. We prep for visits from his five-year-old brother, Ian, by "de-Ian-izing," the house, thus protecting that which concerns us.

Okay, so *House Beautiful* isn't in my future. The kids are grown, so maybe it's time for a new career. How about doing what I've always dreamed of doing? Scuba diving! *Yes, I'm one crab short of a full net.* My heart races when I think about gliding through the ocean depths and romping with dolphins. Then I look at my past-middle-aged flab and say, "I … don't … think … so."

Maybe it's time to give my *Make Believe* world to Jesus and simply believe in Him.

Prayer Pathway: *Jesus, may my joy in knowing You outshine the glitter this world has to offer.*

New in the News

Scripture Trail: Lamentations 3:22-24, Luke 2:10, Philippians 4:8

Stepping Stone: Philippians 4:8

> *"Finally, brethren ... whatever things are of good report, if there is any virtue and if there is anything praiseworthy—think on these things."*

Newspapers seldom provide a great place to get a feel-good fix. ***Unemployment rates climb again.*** And how about this: ***Inflation outstrips cost of living***.

In this week's news, gas prices exceed four dollars a gallon. Not good for those with limited incomes. So and so has been arrested for robbery, hit and run, child abuse, embezzlement, and the list goes on. In my home state of Oregon, prisoners get released early because of overcrowding.

All of this information is way past the pull date. I would do a double take if I saw headlines take a new direction. Someday, I'd like to see positive stories filling tomorrow's newspaper.

Forget burying good news on the back page of Section D. Copy editors of the world, try these news flashes on for size:

Volunteers—pillars of cancer support networking. Just a phone call away, cancer survivors provide a listening ear, answer questions, and give encouragement, day or night.

Elderly live life to the fullest. Senior adults, enduring chronic pain, serve as surrogate grandparents to underprivileged children, deliver Meals on Wheels to shut-ins, and lead city councils.

Blue collar workers—the backbone of our nation. What would our streets look like without garbage collectors? How long would businesses run without electricians, carpet cleaners, plumbers, and taxi drivers? How would we cope without grocery clerks, busboys, and baristas?

What if Jesus were the editor of the paper? His headline declared: **Good tidings of great joy—to all people**. Now that's news worth reading.

Prayer Pathway: *May I focus on the good—rather than the bad and the ugly.*

User Friendly?

Scripture Trail: Proverbs 9:9, Proverbs 11:2, Matthew 18: 3-5

Stepping Stone: Proverbs 11:2

> *"When pride comes, then comes shame; but with the humble is wisdom."*

A computer whiz, I am not. Fortunately, I married one. I would not push the ON button were it not for my resident expert. When it comes to making a computer mess up, I win first prize.

Although I am *Computer* challenged, I appreciate their capabilities, to the extent my limited intellect allows. I even feel deprived when my screen freezes—something like my TV blacking out at the best part of a movie. Despite my sincere efforts to extol the marvels of technology, I confess: *computers hurt my pride.*

When I sat down to write this amazing dissertation, I noticed my taskbar was missing. *Taskbar ... hmmm, how's that for high-tech terminology?* Hearing me grumble, my son nonchalantly waltzed into my office and offered to see if he could fix my problem. Robert did so in about twenty seconds.

In my mind, that was a twenty-dollar fix. At that rate, he earned nigh-on to thirty-six hundred bucks an hour. I reckon I won't show this devotional to him any time soon.

Back to the pride issue. Robert flies through cyberspace as easily as I devour books. He even understands the spaghetti of wires that comes with hooking up a system. I'm content with knowing how to use a mouse to control the beady little cursor that helps me create and fix all my blunders.

Could it be there are many things I can learn from the younger generation? *Undoubtedly ... positutely ... for sure.*

Prayer Pathway: *Lord, I'm willing and ready to learn new things from young sprouts. Bring them on!*

Drawing a Blank

Scripture Trail: Psalm 90:17, Habakkuk 2:2, 1 Corinthians 2:9-10

Stepping Stone: Habakkuk 2:2

> *"Then the LORD answered me … 'Write the vision and make it plain on tablets, that he may run who reads it.'"*

"Oh, wow! A blank page!" Some writers rub their palms together as they poise their fingers over the computer keys, eager to let their thoughts flow onto the screen. Their eyes dance. Steam rises from their ears, as their mental wheels whir.

"Oh, no … a blank page." Madam writer sits with her fingers suspended in space, ready to hear clicking keys. Nothing comes. I rest a hand over my heart. *Yep, it's still beating.* My chest rises and falls., Oxygen's reaching my pea brain. *Whew … not sure there for a minute.*

I wonder if the Bible scribes ever experienced writer's block. After all, The Holy Spirit inspired them. As they leaned over their scrolls, did they vacillate between words pouring forth from their quill, to sweat dripping from their temples over finding the *perfect word*? Did John the Revelator ever stop cold and scratch his head?

God used holy men of old to capture His message on blank slates and papyrus. Nowadays, this saint (God's word, not mine) sits down at a blank computer screen instead of unrolling parchment scrolls. With all my highfalutin technology, nothing I write could hold a candle to the pages penned by Moses and the Apostle Paul.

And yet, the psalmist David … a shepherd boy, belched and sneezed—like me. I connect the dots. Renewed hope wells up within me as I seek the same Holy Spirit who guided ordinary vessels to pen His Holy Word. His ink well never runs dry.

Prayer Pathway: *God, what a relief that You want my availability more than my ability.*

Hot Chocolate

Scripture Trail: Job 37:5-7, Proverbs 25:13, Isaiah 55:10

Stepping Stone: Isaiah 55:10

> *"For as the rain comes down and the snow from heaven, and do not return there, but water the earth … that it may give seed to the sower and bread to the eater."*

Snow swirled and whirled, performing a beautiful dance outside my living room window. Trees and shrubs showed off their newest garb of white. Children romped and laughed in delight in their gigantic playpen of glistening fluff. With time off from school, snowball fights became the order of the day, mixed with laughter and a few tears when a cold missile hit a younger child too hard.

During the night, while I slept, the snow stopped falling, leaving behind a twinkling tapestry of powdery crystals. Early this morning the white blanket covering the ground remains fresh and unspoiled. From my view, not even a dog's paw print or a car's tread interrupts the pristine purity of the landscape. And now I sit sipping hot chocolate as I revel in The Creator's handiwork. The scene outside suggests a picture perfect postcard. Inside my cozy house, I snuggle in a soft blanket and enjoy a special wintertime treat of steaming cocoa.

Relaxing with a cup of hot chocolate in one hand, and a pen and paper in the other, makes me a happy camper. While I wrap my fingers around a warm mug and write my thoughts at my leisure, the world becomes a delightful place.

When God made cocoa beans, He surely had snowy days in mind. After He created this pleasing duo of frosty fluff and makings for warm chocolate, perhaps He laughed while His kids stuffed snowballs down each other's neck. Snow ice cream anyone?

Prayer Pathway: *What a blessing that You fill even long winter days with beauty, warmth, and fun.*

His Princess

Scripture Trail: Isaiah 61:10, Ezekiel 16:8-10, Revelation 7:9

Stepping Stone: Revelation 7:9

> *"... behold, a great multitude which no one could number ... standing before the throne and before the Lamb, clothed with white robes ..."*

Mama hung up our pretty new dresses, one on each side of the door frame leading into the living room. Whether we brought home new clothes for school, for Easter, or for Christmas, my sister, Patty, and I admired our girly frills. When we donned our new clothing, we danced and twirled like Cinderella at the ball.

Now a generation later, my two granddaughters, Elena and Lauren, carry on the feminine tradition that comes with ruffles and lace. By age 3, they already knew the drill. Their mommies did not have to teach them how to whirl and twirl. Now 8, their sweet princess eyes still dance with delight when they model their pretties.

Little girls grow into big girls and not much changes. Instead of promenading for my parents, I model my latest find for my captive audience of one. My husband's flirtatious grin makes me feel like his princess. I chuckle at his loving approval.

What is it about new clothes that transforms my emotions? Perhaps the idea that no one else has worn the garment makes me feel special. The crisp fabric speaks of freshness and beauty.

I smile at the memories of shopping with Mama. Our mother/daughter sprees hark back to a rite of passage that ushered me from childhood to womanhood.

My heavenly Father, nodding His approval, offers me royal robes of righteousness. He drapes His priceless gift on my shoulders. Clothed in dazzling white, I rejoice in my King's delight.

Prayer Pathway: *Father, how humbled I am that You would clothe me in the robe of Your righteousness.*

A fresh and vibrant faith...how might this look for me?

I lay every burden and joy at the feet of Jesus.

"How astounding that God looks past my junk and sees riches."

Time Passing

Half a century and more I've seen
The passing of the years
Some were filled with pleasure
And some were filled with tears

Even teardrops glisten
Like raindrops in the light
Or sometimes fall unnoticed
In the darkness of the night

Each drop could teach a lesson
In the changing ways of life
Or in silence I may wonder
'Til a smile tells me what's right

Dark hair that's silver-frosted
And eyes with memories glow
Going on to more tomorrows
Where do tomorrows go?

Written by Leota Littleton (1957)
Nora's mother

Walking in Love

Steps

"Are we there yet?"

"You WHAT?"

Second Moms

"Never!"

A 'Perfect 7'

An Apple a Day

"Caught ya!"

Lovebursts

A Mother's Love

'Til Death Do Us Part

Mollie's Box

Lifted by Love
Poem

*"By this all will know that you are My disciples,
if you have love for one another."
John 13:35*

19

"Are we there yet?"

Scripture Trail: Matthew 15:24, Luke 19:9-10, 1 Corinthians 13:4

Stepping Stone: 1 Corinthians 13:4

"Love suffers long and is kind ..."

Celebrating our silver wedding anniversary, Arlen and I traveled to the Oregon coast. How well I remember my big kid whining, "Are we there yet?" Parents expect this tune from tired-of-the-car six-year-olds. I just don't know what his problem was. We had only driven a measly two hours beyond our planned schedule.

When we left for our *short* trip, my trusting spouse made one fatal error; he designated me 'navigator'. Note: *his error*. What was my man thinking when he handed the map to his directionally-challenged wife?

Lincoln City occupies a grand total of 5.3 square miles. One would think that even the most inept guide could find a target that size. It's not like I was looking for an obscure street.

My problem? Some cartographer designated a landmass of 992 square miles a county. Back in the day before GPS gizmos, this mapmaker, who loved the name *Lincoln*, labeled this wondrous hunk of terra firma *Lincoln County*. Then he went one step further, and in teensy-weensy letters added *Lincoln City*, along with a bazillion other towns.

Now, how was I supposed to correctly find his microscopic inscription among the wrinkles of the unfolded paper that I clutched in my hands? We didn't do too badly, other than doubling our driving time on that *dark and stormy night.* Can we say *monsoon*?

Now, Arlen, repeat after me:

"Love is patient ... I love my wife ... love is very patient ... I *really really* do love my wife ..."

Prayer Pathway: *Father, help me to always remember that love is spelled P-A-T-I-E-N-C-E.*

"You WHAT?"

Scripture Trail: 1 Corinthians 13:4-7, Galatians 5:22, 1 John 1:9

Stepping Stone: 1 Corinthians 13:5

> *"[Love] does not behave rudely, does not seek its own, is not provoked, thinks no evil."*

"I did a bad thing." My husband avoided eye contact as he stood dangling an electrical cord in front of my face. With his best *I-didn't-mean-to-do-it* expression, his lower lip quivered. "I … umm … accidentally … unplugged your computer."

Arlen's dramatic appeal for mercy fell on stony ground; inside I was thinking, "You WHAT?" *And right in the middle of when I'm writing a devotional!* How's that for Miss Spiritual?

My own sense of the dramatic kicked in, but in not-so-cute form. A stage director could have cast me in a couple of leading roles. Try the wounded woman, the back of her hand against her forehead, ready to faint from shock. Or worse yet, how about the starring role of Rocky, poised to emotionally deck my sweetie?

Oh, my. Forgive me, Lord … forgive me, Arlen. Somehow, I don't think God's work will come to a grinding halt if I never write another word. However, my frustration, verging on anger, could have caused lasting hurt.

After I repented in sackcloth and ashes to God and to my husband, Arlen gently squeezed my hands. With contrite puppy dog eyes, he admitted he'd set me up *just a tad* when he walked in with the disconnected cord. My techie knew the computer had automatically saved most of my work. He also knew his computer-challenged wife wasn't privy to such panic-saving information.

Nevertheless, I forgave Arlen. He forgave me. God forgave us both. Thanks to His mercy, life is good.

Prayer Pathway: *Lord, help me be slow to anger and quick to forgive … even when I'm set up to blow up.*

Second Moms

Scripture Trail: Ruth 1:16, Psalm 113:9, Titus 2:3-5

Stepping Stone: Titus 2:3

> *"the older women likewise, that they be reverent in behavior, not slanderers, not given to much wine, teachers of good things—"*

Second moms rank high on the list of indispensable people in my life. Although my wonderful unofficial mothers now walk the streets of gold, memories of their selfless love keeps me going. With tender, but enthusiastic encouragement, they dared me to not limit 'the possible' in my life.

My *first* second mom came on the scene when I was just a young tyke. My eldest sister, Minnie Belle, her husband, and their three sons, moved from Texas to the farm where I grew up in Oregon. Sis faithfully took me to church and made it possible for me to meet Jesus. When I was a teenager, she modeled how to teach children in Sunday school. I could call on her, day or night.

Doris opened her home to me, a love-struck teenager. She welcomed me into her family so that I could remain near my military sweetheart. Her exuberant love for Jesus led me to worship and rejoice as a daughter of The King. Doris left behind five daughters, unofficial sisters who mean the world to me.

Bonita didn't know a stranger. Deaf from birth and nonverbal, she imparted confidence that, to this day, inspires me to step outside my comfort zone. The local super mall became her second home. Trusty pencil and paper in hand, she hobnobbed with store clerks and shoppers. Bonita caught a city bus almost daily, refusing to limit her world. She taught me to not limit mine.

Second moms—second fiddle to none.

Prayer Pathway: *Lord, please use me as a second mom to young people who need a mother's embrace.*

"Never!"

Scripture Trail: Proverbs 19:21, Proverbs 27:1, James 4:13-15

Stepping Stone: James 4:15

> *"Instead you ought to say, 'If the Lord wills, we shall live and do this or that.'"*

Never say, "Never!"

When I was a young girl, I tagged along for grocery shopping with my big sister, Laurie, who had four children. She also cooked for the hired hands on the farm, so her shopping carts overflowed when she reached the only checkout counter in her tiny rural store. I shook my head and vowed I would *never* have to spend my money to buy that much food. Now, after seven children, numerous foster children, their friends, and frequent guests, I've had to 'eat' my words.

As a young mother, I spoke my *Never!* declaration to more than one willing listener. When the topic of foster care came up, my knee jerk response was "Never!" I couldn't imagine parting with children, so I would *never* do foster care. Subject closed. Then the couple next door separated, the plan being to send their children three different directions. How could I watch them lose their parents and each other as well?

In order to get financial assistance for a larger family, Arlen and I became certified foster parents. Time passed, things stabilized between Mom and Dad, and our first foster kids went back home. Amazingly, I survived the sadness and loss of saying goodbye.

Then another crisis situation developed involving two children we already knew. Once again, the opportunity to foster parent appeared. After five foster children had come and gone, we were hooked.

Maybe I should learn a new phrase: "Yes, Lord." *Hmm … that has a nice ring.*

Prayer Pathway: *Lord, may I never say, "Never!" to You.*

A 'Perfect 7'

Scripture Trail: Genesis 2:3, Psalm 127:3-5, Galatians 4:5

Stepping Stone: Genesis 2:3

>*"Then God blessed the seventh day and sanctified it ..."*

When Arlen and I began our journey as parents, little did we know that we'd end up with 7, the Bible's number for perfection.

Eddy, our first born, your humility never ceases to bless others. You mirror love, grace, and kindness as naturally as breathing air.

Jim, our second born. Your sense of humor and thoughtfulness continually bless us. Our number one drama king, your laughter lights up our lives.

Larry, our third born. You make life exciting, while never ceasing to amaze us. Keep your passion for pursuing excellence at every turn.

Cory, at four months old we looked at you and we were goners. In hardship, you have modeled courage. We couldn't be more proud of you. And so you became our first adoption miracle.

Reneé, upon your arrival at eight-years-old, we could finally proclaim, "We have a daughter!" What a blessing you are to Dad and to me. The beautiful drawing you gave us, along with your words of thanks for adopting you, still make us cry.

Tyana, again an eight-year-old sweetie, you settled in the Peacock nest. Your kindness, love for God, and perseverance through pain defines the word *inspiration*. You are a priceless treasure.

Bobby, at ten-years-old, you rounded out our perfect 7! With your continued willingness to work hard, you'll realize your dreams. You are a leader, Son, and we see a great future ahead for you.

To our precious 7, through all our joys and tears, you have made us the perfect family.

Prayer Pathway: *Born into Your Spirit ... adopted by You, my Father God. I am overwhelmed.*

An Apple a Day

Scripture Trail: Psalm17:8, Proverbs 7:1-3, Proverbs 25:11

Stepping Stone: Psalm 17:8

> *"Keep me as the apple of Your eye; hide me under the shadow of Your wings."*

I should be the picture of health, but not because I eat an apple a day. What started with a few items of apple décor for my kitchen has bloomed into an orchard. My culinary corner truly *runneth over* with apples.

Apples are a happy fruit. A special story resides in just about every apple I own. From my puppet apple, complete with its own wiggly worm, to a clock with pictures of one more bite of apple gone at each hour, to a sassy-faced apple sitting on my toaster, I delight in my fruity kitchen.

God tells me I am "the apple of His eye." I wonder why He chose the apple to make His point. Somehow, "You are the turnip of my eye," just doesn't cut it. Maybe He knew one of His daughters would revel in the love expressed by the bushels of apples brought to her door.

In the textbooks of American history, a playful tale must hide behind an "Apple for the Teacher." Perhaps some freckle-faced little girl in pigtails charmed her teacher into an extra recess as she held out her shiny red offering.

Jesus invited the little children to come to Him. I can easily imagine His joyful smile as He receives an apple, whether shiny or bruised, from a chubby little hand. And when He did so, THE Master Teacher tousled the child's hair and rubbed the apple offering on His mighty chest as He boasted, "Now, that's *My* kid!"

Prayer Pathway: *I'm so glad that You shelter me in the apple orchard of Your love.*

"Caught ya!"

Scripture Trail: Matthew 6:3, Luke 11:4, Ephesians 5:1-2

Stepping Stone: Ephesians 5:2

> *"And walk in love, as Christ also has loved us and given Himself for us, an offering and a sacrifice to God for a sweet-smelling aroma."*

He wasn't dressed like a cat burglar, even though he rummaged around in my house in the middle of the night. With stealthy movements, the tall *intruder* almost got away with his quiet caper. Then I walked in.

My sleepy eyes took a minute to focus. Even so, I knew the man in my kitchen was my husband. Roses in hand, Arlen looked at me and grinned. His expression spoke his thoughts—*busss … ted!*

Two vases sat on the countertop. I caught my midnight marauder struggling to figure out which vase to use. Arlen's philosophy, *"Why do today what you can put off until tomorrow?"* snagged him once again. With our wedding anniversary just hours away, Arlen's left hand didn't know whether to trade places with his right hand as he sheepishly fumbled to hide his love offering behind his back.

This time I caught my *darlin' Arlen* red-handed and red-faced, holding the rosy evidence. No need to hire Sherlock Holmes.

"For richer, for poorer … for early or late …" Well, we didn't have the "early or late" part in our wedding vows, but we should have. Arlen and I agree that his tardiness is not an aberration. Just for fun, I might even add the *early/late* promise when we renew our vows for our next landmark anniversary. Whether frantically fumbling or Johnny-on-the-spot, I love this man God has given me. Even more astonishing, he still loves me, his *gotta-do-it-yesterday* and *let's-arrive-an-hour-early* wife.

Prayer Pathway: *Help me have a merciful heart toward others, knowing how much I stand in need of mercy.*

Lovebursts

Scripture Trail: Proverbs 20:11, Jeremiah 31:3, 1 John 4:10-12

Stepping Stone: 1 John 4:11

> *"Beloved, if God so loved us, we also ought to love one another."*

Something about grandchildren causes grandmas and grandpas to melt inside like chocolate on a sunny day. Even when I know ahead of time that my grandkids are coming for a visit, my joy barometer spikes when I hear a little fist tap at my door.

All of our grandchildren bless me and my hubby with precious words of love when we see them. Two of our grandsons, Cory and Travis, grew up giving *Oh, buddies!* which translated means *really really tight hugs* with their eyes squeezed shut.

When our oldest grandson, Cory, now 20, was just a little munchkin, he bounded in the door one day, threw his arms around Grandpa's leg, and shouted, "I love you sooo much, Grandpa!"

Enthralled by their *Oh, buddies!* I did not feel ignored at all. Nevertheless, Cory remembered to not leave Grandma out. He turned around, gave me one of his super duper hugs and proclaimed, "I love you too, Grandma!" His younger brother, Travis, was never far behind in blessing us with his special *Oh, buddies!*

Lovebursts ... love given with pure innocence by a child. What could be better? No hidden agendas, no premeditated efforts to manipulate—but simply the deepest affection.

I can hardly wait to one day throw my arms around Jesus and hug Him super duper tight. When I leave behind my adulthood and love on Him like a child, I feel Him hug me right back. His warm embrace—what a great place to stay.

Prayer Pathway: *Are You ready, Jesus? I'm sending You a super duper 'Oh-buddy' right now!*

A Mother's Love

Scripture Trail: 1 Samuel 1:27, John 19:25, 1 Thessalonians 2:7-8

Stepping Stone: 1 Thessalonians 2:7

> *"But we were gentle among you, just as a nursing mother cherishes her own children."*

How many shirts does it take to buy a piano? This is not a trick question as in, "How many _____ does it take to screw in a light bulb?" And there's no need to call in a mathematician with a PhD. Were my mother still here on earth, she could produce a good ballpark figure.

For years Mama worked in a drycleaners and saved her money until one day, with sparkling eyes and a playful grin, she asked me, "How about we go shopping for a piano today?"

Several long seconds passed as I stood weak-kneed and stared at her with my mouth hanging open, unable to respond. While I waited for my world to stop spinning, the need for CPR seemed a distinct possibility.

Now 30 years later, I look at Mama's precious gift and still shake my head in wonder. When I consider the years and countless hours of operating a hot steam press, I still choke up with gratitude for her love. No song played on those beautiful ivories, nor words penned, convey what I find impossible to express.

Such extravagant love. Such selfless sacrifice. I can still see the immeasurable joy radiating from Mom's eyes when she revealed her long-held question.

Just maybe God created a mother's heart to give me a glimpse of His boundless love. From the beginning of time, His perfect plan included one special mama whose love came wrapped in a shirt press and a piano.

Prayer Pathway: *O God of limitless love, You know exactly how to reveal how much I mean to You.*

'Til Death Do Us Part

Scripture Trail: John 15:7, 1 Corinthians 13:7, Ephesians 5:31-33

Stepping Stone: 1 Corinthians 13:7

> *"[Love] bears all things, believes all things, hopes all things, endures all things."*

Wedding bells rang for Lee and Marcia Mitchell on March 1, 1975. They weren't content to settle for just any old bells, so while on their honeymoon they began a bell collection, which eventually numbered more than a thousand. Their special bells included an 1832 Bevin Bell and a Luristan Horse Bell that dates back to the time of King David.

When not busy looking for bells for his belle, Lee built an addition to their house for their blended family. This talented man crafted a leather purse and Bible cover for Marcia, and encouraged her to pursue her writing. He studied to become a building inspector, but by the test date Marcia knew something was terribly wrong. In 1984, just nine years after they said, "I do," Lee was diagnosed with probable Alzheimer's disease.

This man, who loved to bless people, quickly changed. One day Lee slammed the car brakes because he saw a guy with long hair. When he asked Marcia to take him places, he expected her to know ahead of time where he wanted to go. But even in his confusion, he thanked her for putting up with him. Along with mothering their six children, year after year Marcia lovingly took care of Lee even when "for better" turned to "for worse."

Thirty-one years, three months, and two days from their wedding day, heaven's bells welcomed Lee home.

Marcia and Lee's sweet love song still rings out its *'til death do us part* message.

Prayer Pathway: *Lord, thank You for those who teach me how to love—no matter what.*

Mollie's Box

Scripture Trail: Proverbs 31:20, Luke 6:38, John 6:9-13

Stepping Stone: Luke 6:38

> *"Give and it shall be given to you: good measure, pressed down, shaken together, and running over will be put into your bosom ..."*

Mollie's box and Lucille Ball's oven share much in common. In one memorable *I Love Lucy* episode, Lucy put bread dough in a warm oven so the yeast would rise. In typical Lucy fashion, she overdid it on the yeast. Raw dough soon oozed out the oven door and up through the burners. While Lucy's oven disaster produced hilarity, the overflow of Mollie's box generates gratitude.

After innumerable trips by person after person to Mollie's car trunk, the renowned container became known as "Mollie's Box." Her garage of *items for the taking* supplements her legendary *box*. She stands on-the-ready to provide transportation to appointments or to give a list of resources for people's needs. But whatever form Mollie's box takes, the fruit of her giving multiplies like the boys small lunch that Jesus used to feed 5,000 men and their families.

Beds, a roll top desk, a walker, a shoehorn with a three-foot handle, and payment of electric bills include just a fraction of the items pouring forth from Mollie's 'box'. When she opened her wonder-working care package of compassion to a needy teenager, the young girl soon discovered the love of Jesus and then led her drug dealer to the Lord.

Behind this amazing woman stands a great man who hauls boxes, furniture, and whatever his ambitious wife needs delivered to someone's doorstep. Like the boys lunch, Jesus multiplies Carl's and Mollie's fixed income—His response to willing hands, ready and available for The Master's miracles.

Prayer Pathway: *Jesus, may I never put limits on what You wish to accomplish through me.*

My love letter to Jesus:

_____

_____

_____

_____

_____

_____

_____

_____

_____

_____

_____

_____

_____

_____

_____

I lay every burden and joy at the feet of Jesus.

"I can
hardly wait
to one day throw my
arms around Jesus
and hug Him
super duper
tight."

Lifted by Love

When weakness o'erwhelms me
Your love you share
With servant's hands
And hearts that care

    And I am lifted by your arms
        into His arms of love

When hope eludes me
Midst skies of gray
With faith's assurance
For me, you pray

    And I am lifted by your arms
        into His arms of love

When fears oppress me
His peace He sends
With compassion's call
Through you, my friends

    And I am lifted by your arms
        into His arms of love

    And there—I am healed

Written for Carl and Mollie Clark
Thank you for your ministry
of love and sacrifice.

Standing ... I Wait

Steps

Can't Wait!

The Golden Goose that Didn't

Just Expecting

"Anybody home?"

"Over here!"

Sounds in the Night

"It's spring!"

60 Seconds to Eternity

Wannabe Writer

"Can you hear me now?"

Waiting

Close to His Heart
Poem

*"Wait on the LORD; be of good courage,
and He shall strengthen your heart;
wait, I say, on the LORD!" Psalm 27:14*

Can't Wait!

Scripture Trail: Psalm 62:5, Isaiah 30:18, Lamentations 3:22-27

Stepping Stone: Psalm 62:5

> *"My soul, wait silently for God alone, for my*
> *expectation is from Him."*

The old farmhouse I grew up in had a large country kitchen with an old-fashioned box refrigerator. This white monolith stood maybe a whopping five-feet high. As a young girl, I couldn't wait to stand as tall as our dear old icebox. While waiting for my refrigerator height to hurry up and happen, I also couldn't wait to become a cool teenager like my big brother, Larry.

Then one day I woke up and, "Voilá!" I'd morphed into a pimple-faced creature with long skinny legs. Unbelievably, a severe case of 'I-can't-wait to hear wedding bells' soon eclipsed my adolescent joy. When would I ever find my prince charming? At the ripe old age of 15 my tall, dark, and handsome prince showed up. Then when I hit the *mature* age of 18, I stepped across the threshold of blissful matrimony and said, "I do."

Of course, nothing would do but to find another focus for my anticipation. Babies! *Big surprise.* Not many years passed before little 'peachicks' filled my nest.

For much of my adult life I've bounced from one *can't wait* to the next: the next college course, the next women's retreat, the next child's wedding, the next perfect 10 grandchild. My cup overfloweth with *can't wait* milestones.

As a graying granny, my *hurry-upper* got up and went some time ago. While my body ages, forcing me to slow *down*, I'm learning to savor the *now* moments. When I wait on Him, I find His presence more than enough.

Prayer Pathway: *Teach me, Lord, to slow down enough to hear*
You speak to me.

The Golden Goose that Didn't

Scripture Trail: Job 6:20, Psalm 16:5, Matthew 6:19-21

Stepping Stone: Job 6:20

> *"They are disappointed because they were confident;*
> *they come there and are confused."*

A new pair of shoes! Butterflies did a happy dance inside my tummy. No ordinary run-of-the-mill stompers for this kid. I just *'had to have' Red Goose* shoes that came with a proverbial *golden egg*. I dreamed about the promised treasures hidden inside.

The big day finally came when Mama and I searched the store's shoe racks. I cared far more about getting my golden egg than I did the contents of the shoebox I carried to the register. I'd soon have my reward for my hours of giddy daydreaming.

Mom paid for my shoes and then the store clerk reached below the counter to retrieve my riches. Alas! No eggs! *How could it be? I* scarcely heard the clerk's apology and assurance that we could come back later and claim my jackpot.

Later never came. My tender spirit felt so crushed that one would have thought my pet bunny had died. I have no memory of what the shoes looked like. I only remember burying my tear-streaked face in Mama's fuzzy sweater.

I'm a big girl now. The memory no longer stings. Instead, I chuckle at the little girl who cried over cheap trinkets.

I'd like to think I've grown up and that I no longer allow disappointment to overwhelm me. Well, I guess I'm still pondering the *grown up* part. I don't always shake off disappointment. But I'm working on it. Fifty-some years ago the Golden Goose blew it.

And guess what. It's okay. It's really okay.

Prayer Pathway: *When my dreams end in disappointment, thank You, Father, for healing my wounded heart.*

Just Expecting

Scripture Trail: Isaiah 40:29-31, Jeremiah 1:5, Romans 8:16

Stepping Stone: Jeremiah 1:5

> *"Before I formed you in the womb, I knew you ..."*

Papa Peacock and I rejoiced each time we expected a little one. With each baby, Arlen shared my eagerness to confirm that a new little *Peachick* was on the way. Back in the *olden days*, women went to the doctor to get pregnancy test results.

By the third child, Arlen planned to wait until after work to find out if he would become a daddy again. To my delight, he couldn't wait until his workday ended. He surprised me by showing up at the doctor's office to hear the good news. Another patient assumed we were first-time parents, our joy was so great.

During my first two pregnancies, job changes moved us cross country. When eating out at restaurants, our standard order included a glass of milk and a cup of coffee. The servers, noticing my *delicate condition*, invariably gave me the milk and Arlen the coffee. Daddy-in-waiting enjoyed switching beverages, commenting to the server, "I'm not pregnant, just expecting!"

Soon after baby number three fluttered in my stomach, I bought Arlen a custom-lettered T-shirt. The front said, "Paging Papa Peacock." The back boasted his favorite line, "I'm not pregnant, just expecting!" He wore it often during the months of waiting for our third son's birth.

One other expectant parent breathlessly waits in the wings. What does a God-size celebration look like? When I asked Him to become my Abba Father, did He shout: "Kill the fatted calf! Clang the cymbals! Sound the trumpets! I'm a papa again!"

Prayer Pathway: *Abba Father, I'm so glad You're my Daddy God.*

"Anybody home?"

Scripture Trail: Matthew 24:42, Mark 13:35-36, Titus 2:13

Stepping Stone: Matthew 24:42

> *"Watch therefore, for you know neither the day nor the hour in which the Son of Man is coming."*

Jonas pulled in the driveway. The end of another day at the salt mines. He picked up his briefcase and walked into the house. *What's with all the lights on? Why's the TV blaring ... again? Emma shouldn't put up with this.* The vacuum cleaner droned.

He cleared his throat. "I'm home!" *Maybe Emma ran upstairs to deal with fussy girls. Still, she could at least take a second to shut down our humming Hoover.*

Jonas walked through the house. "Anybody home?" *Maybe my babe's getting dolled up for dinner. That's it. She's sent the kids to the neighbors.* He tiptoed to their half-open bedroom door. *Quiet ... too quiet.* He went to the bedroom window. Ned's and Celia's cars were in their driveway. *Good.* Grabbing his cell, he hit speed dial.

Ned answered. "Haven't seen 'em. Toilet's flooding." Click.

Jonas raked his fingers through his hair. *Did Jesus come?* He yelled again. No answer. *Did the Rapture happen and I got left behind?* A moment later, car doors slammed and two giggling daughters tumbled into the house, followed by Emma, grocery bags in hand. He met her at the door and in his best nonchalant voice asked, "Sooo ... who's been minding the Hoover?"

"We had a power outage. The store was a madhouse." Emma shook her head. "You'd think it was the end of the world."

Jonas turned off the vacuum cleaner. *Whew, I didn't miss God's trumpet call.* (Names changed to protect ... you know the drill.)

Prayer Pathway: *Lord, may I always be ready for Your return.*

"Over here!"

Scripture Trail: Proverbs 2:1-5, Romans 8:39, Ephesians 2:14

Stepping Stone: Ephesians 2:14

> *"For He Himself is our peace, who has made both one, and has broken down the middle wall of separation,"*

Meeting friends for lunch makes my day. Lynn and I picked our date, time, and place: Thursday noon, at a restaurant midway between our homes. Arriving early, I found a table where I wouldn't miss seeing her walk in. Usually this strategy works great ... *except.* I saw a flashing reader board in my future: *Warning ... senior moment coming ... senior moment coming.*

My friend, Miss Reliable, arrived early as well—*before* I did. Two cups of coffee later, I wondered if I'd written down the wrong date. Lynn would surely call me if she were caught in traffic.

Ten minutes passed, then twenty. If she didn't arrive soon, I'd have a caffeine buzz that would curl my hair. Twenty-five minutes ticked by. Now I was really getting worried. Was she lying unconscious in a ditch somewhere, bleeding to death?

After waiting a half hour, an over-worked angel must have pulled the cord to the light bulb in my brain. *I wonder ... do you suppose ... I doubt it, but then just maybe ... no way. She couldn't be on the other side of the divider, could she?*

I got up and peeked around the corner. *Sure enough.* Relieved and more than a little embarrassed, we considered offering our rosy-cheeked mugs for a new TV program called, "Dumb People Tricks."

Lynn knew where she was. I knew where I was. Not knowing where our 'wuzzes' were, we almost missed out on bodacious calorie-free peach cobbler ... ala mode!

Prayer Pathway: *Jesus, I ask You to break down every wall that would separate me from You.*

Sounds in the Night

Scripture Trail: 1 Kings 19:11-12, Psalm 95:7, Acts 22:14

Stepping Stone: 1 Kings 19:12

> *"and after the earthquake a fire, but the LORD was not in the fire; and after the fire a still small voice."*

Tonight a frog croaks outside my window. Its throaty sound sends my thoughts back to days on the farm catching the small critters with my sister, Patty. She even tried to smuggle a little green toad to school by telling Mama that she kept her hands in her pockets because they were cold. Mom caught on quick. The tiny frog stayed home.

A ticking clock on the wall behind me reminds me of a time when Arlen spent the night on my parents' couch. The cuckoo clock's little bird faithfully popped out once on every half hour, and predictably up to twelve times on the hour, until midnight. The naughty bird then restarted its hourly pronouncements, marking one to twelve. Arlen looked worn-out the next morning—*go figure*.

The furnace just turned on. Growing up, how many different heaters did Mom and Dad use, trying to heat the old farmhouse? Patty and I huddled close on cold mornings as we jumped into our school clothes. We competed for warmth in a small area filled with drying racks of wet laundry. Those chilly memories with my kid sister make me smile now.

There's one more sound in the night that I must stay quiet to hear. The hushed voice of The Holy Spirit reminds me that I have much to be thankful for. No matter yesterday's challenges, His presence hovered nearby through each circumstance of my life.

His still small voice in the night … the sweetest sound of all.

Prayer Pathway: *Jesus, I want to push aside any distraction that would prevent me from hearing Your voice.*

"It's spring!"

Scripture Trail: Deuteronomy 11:13-15, Isaiah 42:9, Joel 2:23

Stepping Stone: Deuteronomy 11:14

> *"then I will give you the rain for your land in its season, the early rain and the latter rain, that you may gather in your grain, your new wine ..."*

Summer sunshine fills a cloudless blue sky, golden autumn leaves present a fiery display, and winter snow glistens in all its purity. Nevertheless, spring takes first prize.

When January begins, I start pestering friends, family, and strangers with, "Guess what ... spring starts month after next!" On the first day of February, I tug the closest person's sleeve and exclaim, "Next month, spring is here!" People must tire of my frequent announcements. Indulgent smiles greet my proclamations that herald the advent of this spectacular season of the year.

Baby birds in their nests chirp, "Feed me! Feed me!" Spring rains cleanse the air. I inhale the fragrance of fresh-mown grass. Crocuses, tulips, and daffodils brighten lifeless ground with splashes of color; April showers *do* bring May flowers!

Songwriters sing ballads about love filing the air in springtime. The half-serious slogan among the students at a nearby Bible college states, "A ring by spring, or your money back." They call the pink tree blossoms around campus "the pink mist." A soft blanket of delicate petals covers the grass within reach of each flower-laden branch. An article in the college newspaper, which I read with my very own eyes, reports that a "ring by spring" comes as a direct result of the *pink mist*. It's in writing ... so it must be true!

Spring shouts new life at every turn. Easter programs celebrate resurrection life. New life in nature. New life in The Spirit.

Rah! Rah! Let's hear it for spring!

Prayer Pathway: *Lord, in every season of my life, may my love for You blossom with freshness and beauty.*

60 Seconds to Eternity

Scripture Trail: Luke 12:40, John 3:15-16, Psalm 116:15

Stepping Stone: Psalm 116:15

> *"Precious in the sight of the LORD is the death of His saints."*

People walked between cars and chatted with strangers. Looking at his watch, a young man swore, then climbed on top of his car and took a picture of the stalled freeway, turned parking lot.

Children skipped around while they enjoyed the novelty of this experience. Wives gave husbands irritated glances as their macho men took charge, turning their cars the wrong way on the shoulder to drive back to the top of the entrance ramp. After a police car passed me, I wondered if any determined escapists found another officer camped at the ramp's entrance, ticket book in hand.

An ambulance inched its way around bumper-to-bumper traffic, while drivers nudged their cars to the right and to the left to allow the vehicle to pass. Its flashing red lights reminded me how little this inconvenience mattered. Judging by the number of emergency units on the scene, someone or *someones* up ahead were likely facing eternity.

An hour later, snarled traffic began crawling forward. Whatever I had planned for the evening seemed unimportant. About a mile up the road, I saw a smashed pickup truck and a completely demolished convertible. The car's frame had been crushed down to the seats, every window shattered.

At freeway speed, my son and I missed punching in on eternity's time clock by maybe a minute. Had traffic moved normally, we would have covered that mile in 60 seconds. Someone else's appointed time had come. I pray they awoke to angel song.

Prayer Pathway: *When I must wait, I will trust Your purpose.*

Wannabe Writer

Scripture Trail: Psalm 56:8, Malachi 3:16-17, Hebrews 12:2

Stepping Stone: Psalm 56:8

> *"You number my wanderings; put my tears into Your bottle; are they not in Your book?"*

Most writers harbor a carefully guarded secret that they divulge to only a chosen few. *Someday I will write 'The Great Novel'—the capstone to all my professional aspirations.*

For years, my family has put up with the mood swings of their wannabe writer. One day I'm in tears wailing, "I can't do this!" The next day I'm grinning over an unexpected burst of inspiration that just flowed from my fingertips. When one of my characters dies, I get depressed. That admission demands a rolling of the eyes from someone out there.

As I see the end in sight for my *novel* efforts, I think about Jesus creating everything from nothing. I don't believe He ever beat His holy head against a brick wall over how to express Himself. He never had a case of Creator's block.

From the first glimmer of His creation in Genesis, to the last period at the end of Revelation, He knows the end from the beginning. Not a person or a plant, an animal or an amoeba, happened without Him. He knows the answers before I can ask my questions. He's never had a panic attack over when or if He'll finish what He started.

Whether my 'masterpiece' ever gets a nod from a publisher, Jesus— The Author and Finisher of my faith—holds close my tears, my frustrations, and my joys. With that assurance, I can lay down my quill and leave the results in His holy hands.

Prayer Pathway: *Jesus, whether my dreams are hidden or not-so-secret, I know they are safe with You.*

"Can you hear me now?"

Scripture Trail: 2 Samuel 22:2-4, Job 42:4, Jeremiah 33:3

Stepping Stone: Jeremiah 33:3

> *"Call on Me, and I will answer you, and show you great and mighty things, which you do not know."*

These young whippersnappers expect me to talk to some fake robot voice? I listened intently to the computer-generated instructions. "If you want to disconnect or start service, push the 1 on your telephone keypad. For change of address, push the 2 key." I harrumphed and waited for the next monotone command: "To make a payment, push 3."

Now I'm getting somewhere. Okay … tap the 3 key.

"To pay by debit, push the 1 key, to pay by electronic check push the 2 key." Oops! My finger slipped down and hit a 5 key. "Sorry that is an invalid entry. To go back to the main menu, hit the star key."

"I just want to talk to a human being!" I shouted out loud to no one and then slammed down the phone.

Dare I start over? *Ain't no hi-tech stuff gonna stop this old lady.* The crows' feet at the corners of my eyes stretched tight as my eyeballs bulged with frustration at the tinny message that followed: "Sorry our offices are closed. Please call back between the hours of 8 a.m. to 5 p.m. Eastern Standard Time."

What! I just spent thirty minutes punching buttons and sitting on hold, just to find out I live on the wrong coast? Forget it! Slam. Embarrassed, I breathed a sigh of relief that some upstart computer guru hadn't heard my first, or my second, outburst to thin air.

Hello. Are you there, God? It's just me with egg on my face.

Prayer Pathway: *God, when I call on You, I so appreciate that You patch me right through.*

Waiting

Scripture Trail: Psalm 27:13, Lamentations 3:26, Romans 8:24-25

Stepping Stone: Psalm 27:13

> *"I would have lost heart, unless I had believed that I would see the goodness of the LORD in the land of the living."*

Waiting … something I don't do well … seems a waste of time. So here I sit at a bus station, waiting for friends who haven't arrived as scheduled. They probably missed connections and will arrive on the next bus—two hours from now. The drive home is too far to be worth the round trip, so here I sit and sip coffee.

Other people, like me, are waiting too. Some will connect with friends and family who are excited to see them. A few simply wait for another long day to end.

An elderly man, who appears homeless, lies stretched out on the floor asleep with a newspaper on his face. Another man paces back and forth in the bus terminal conversing with some invisible companion. A feeble old gentleman left the ladies restroom just ahead of me, oblivious to his error.

As I wait for two tedious hours to end, I stave off boredom by expressing my thoughts on paper. Knowing that another bus will show up with my expected guests aboard makes my wait worthwhile. But what about the guy asleep on the floor, the confused person babbling to imagined listeners, and the sweet old man who can't read the restroom signs? I hurt for them.

So humanity waits for something better—no, not for *something*, but for *Someone* better, The Friend who will never leave them friendless. How blessed I am to know The One for whom I wait! *Even so, come quickly, Lord Jesus.*

Prayer Pathway: *Use me, Lord, to show a lonely and lost world how to find their way to You.*

In what areas of my life is Jesus asking me to stop and wait upon Him?

I lay every burden and joy at the feet of Jesus.

"So
humanity
waits for something
better—no, not for
something, but for
Someone better,
The Friend who will
never leave them
friendless."

Close to His Heart

Jesus, tiny babe
Safe in your mother's embrace
Held close to her heart
Did you coo at stumbling calves,
Dear Lamb of God?

Jesus, young man
Guided by Joseph's strong hands
Held close to his heart
Did your fingers trace splintered wood
Dear Son of Man?

Jesus, man grown
Reflection of Abba God's love
Held close to His heart
Did your spirit yearn for His holy arms
Dear Son of God?

Lamb of God
Son of Man
Sent by God for me

Dedicated to my Savior,
whose extravagant love for me
nailed Him to the cross

Puddle Jumping in My Galoshes

Steps

Lemonade Stand—"Open"

Flying Trampoline!

Grinding to a Halt

"OOPS!"

Zippin' the Lip

Lost and Found

A Light in the Window

"A mouse ... in my house?"

Genius at Work

Over-the-top Days

Called to Comfort

Along the Way
Poem

"For lo, the winter is past, the rain is over and gone."
Song of Solomon 2:11

Lemonade Stand—"Open"

Scripture Trail: Psalm 27:13, Psalm 34:8, John 4:13-14

Stepping Stone: John 4:14

> *"but whosoever drinks of the water that I shall give him will never thirst ..."*

"When life gives you lemons, make lemonade." My computer tells me that *Anonymous* coined this familiar quote. If I ever discover the hidden identity of its author, I'll gladly give credit where credit is due.

With lots of people in my life to love, I rejoice in their victories and grieve for their pain. I received a phone call one morning from someone dear to me suffering severe physical and emotional pain. God led me to the Psalms where He took my lemons of despair and squeezed me close, while adding the comforting sweetness of the Holy Spirit to His Word.

His hope poured into me from Psalm 27:13: "I would have lost heart, unless I had believed that I would see the goodness of the LORD in the land of the living." The last phrase flashed like a strobe light off the page.

His hope is for me and for those I love, not just in heaven, but also for here and now *"in the land of the living."*

When I can't *make lemonade* from lemons of pain and sorrow, Jesus steps up to the stand and offers me His soothing reassurance. How grateful I am to the One who knows just what I need to quench my thirst and renew my strength.

When I spend time with Him, I *"taste and see that the Lord is good."* (Psalm 34:8) From His lemonade stand, open 24-7, He offers me a free glass and says, "Drink up!"

Prayer Pathway: *Lord, thank You for Your refreshing comfort that gives me hope and strength.*

Flying Trampoline!

Scripture Trail: Matthew 7:24-25, Mark 4:39, John 3:8

Stepping Stone: Mark 4:39

> *"Then He arose and rebuked the wind, and said to the sea, 'Peace be still!' and the wind ceased and there was a great calm."*

"It's a bird … it's a plane … no, wait. It's a trampoline!"

On a warm summer day I stood outside on our deck, resting my arms on the wood railing. Arlen busied himself with assembling a swing set for our grandchildren. On this sunny afternoon, our family time seemed picture perfect.

I quickly shifted mental gears when a small, but intense, twister whirled across our property. Touching down near my handyman, the winds flipped his heavy toolbox, spilling tools onto the ground.

Before I could worry about Arlen's safety, this frenzied funnel lifted our full-sized trampoline into the air, sending it flying like a giant Frisbee across the field, where springs and metal legs littered its flight path. Our flying saucer finally crashed against a lone tree.

Arlen later said that, as he watched this bizarre scene, he struggled over whether to get upset about the probable loss of his $200 investment. Realizing he didn't have much say in the matter, he stood back and enjoyed the strange spectacle that soared over his head. Instead of letting the winds blow him away, Arlen chose to go with the flow. He did not allow the unexpected and crazy circumstance to ruin his day.

A scavenger hunt through our field later yielded enough springs and metal legs to rebuild our vagabond toy. A few hammer taps and twists of the wrist reshaped the frame, and our UFO landed on its feet again, ready for more years of family fun.

Prayer Pathway: *Help me remember that You don't break a sweat, even in the midst of the fiercest storm.*

Grinding to a Halt

Scripture Trail: Psalm 6:6, Psalm 43:5, Isaiah 40:28-31

Stepping Stone: Psalm 43:5

> *"Why are you cast down, O my soul? And why are you disquieted within me? Hope in God; for I shall yet praise Him, the help of my countenance and my God."*

Does the earth still rotate on its axis when I don't have answers for my children's needs? Will the sun come up tomorrow when I can't accomplish all I wish to as a homemaker and wife? When I can't spread myself thin enough to be there for all of my family and friends in their times of need, does God see my heart? Does He pass me by when the needle for the gas gauge on my spiritual tank buries itself in the red zone?

The minute hand on life's clock ticks on, whether or not I'm at my best. Adult children, with adult-size problems, need God-size solutions. My limited physical energy causes me frequent frustration. My spiritual reservoir goes through seasons of draught.

King David, once a common shepherd boy, became a mighty warrior, commander over armies, and leader of a nation. But his well still ran dry. In despair he spoke firmly to himself, *"Why are you cast down, O my soul? And why are you disquieted within me?"* In our day, I suppose one could say that God's royal servant tweaked his attitude with a reality check, giving himself a swift kick in the pants.

King David likely felt overwhelmed with the demands coming at him from every direction. In comparison, my life seems a cakewalk. Yet this person, identified as a man after God's own heart, reminded himself to place his hope in God.

This shepherd king turned his gaze upward … and so will I.

Prayer Pathway: *When I feel down, please tap me on the shoulder and remind me to look up to You my King.*

"OOPS!"

Scripture Trail: Proverbs 3:5-6, Matthew 6:34, John 14:27

Stepping Stone: Proverbs 3:6

> *"In all your ways acknowledge Him, and He shall direct your paths."*

There's *oops* and then there's *OOPS!* Things like spilled drinks, a typo on a report, stepping on the dog's tail, and a lost nickel fit the *oops* category. Add some minor details and the stakes go way up.

Try a spilled drink that fries a computer keyboard, an added little zero to a sales figure, and a dog that sinks his teeth into his owner's clumsy foot. How about a lost collector's coin from the California Gold Rush? Now I see *OOPS!* written all over the place.

In one of his comedy routines, famed comedian Bill Cosby offered his perspective on the word, "Oops!" He spun a yarn about a surgery patient under local anesthetic who heard the surgeon utter, "Oops!" Poor Bill knew what *he* meant when *he* said, "Oops!" But to overhear his surgeon's declaration … Yikes!

Time has had a way of changing the panic-ridden *OOPS!* moments in my life to *oops* that aren't much more than a blip on my mental radar. *Oops, I forgot to make dessert for tonight's Bible study group.* Oh, well. Somebody has to keep bakeries in business.

So okay, the dessert crisis is no big deal. How about this *OOPS?* I drove off and left my firstborn in the nursery at church. Forty-three years ago, I had a meltdown when I pulled this *OOPS!* All right, I confess. Even now, I would still experience symptoms of cardiac arrest.

Whether I face an *oops* or an *OOPS! God's* always on duty.

Prayer Pathway: *Whether my mistakes are BIG TIME or peanuts, I need You, Father.*

Zippin' the Lip

Scripture Trail: Proverbs 18:21, Matthew 15:18, James 2:2-5

Stepping Stone: Matthew 15:18

> *"But those things which proceed out of the mouth come from the heart, and they defile the man."*

Words. What slippery things. They're harder to control than greased water balloons in a mischievous child's hands. Just when I think I have a grip on the ol' lip, something pops out of my mouth that I wish had not.

The problem of *foot-in-mouth-disease* has been around since Adam and Eve separately tried to pass the buck. A modern rendition of Eve's defensive whining: "Surely my spouse is the louse in this situation." Thus *The Blame Game* began.

In the book of James, Scripture compares the tongue to the rudder of a ship. This tiny part of a vessel determines the course of even large ships. If the rudder isn't functioning properly, the ship may stray off course or run aground.

Studies support what the Bible says about words. Statistics show women speak several thousand more words in a day than men. My husband reaffirms this tidbit of information when he asks me at the end of the day if I've used up all my words. On such occasions, he gets a well-deserved glare from me.

If those studies and statistics prove accurate about women's verbosity, it seems important—especially for us of the female gender—that we turn the rudder of our ship over to God. As I allow Him to cleanse my lips, He will help me avoid verbal shipwreck.

Opportunities to run aground happen daily. Until The Master of the waves declares this vessel seaworthy, I've decided *zippin' the lip* makes a smooth sailing ship.

Prayer Pathway: *Lord, may the words that pass my lips speak life to others at all times.*

Lost and Found

Scripture Trail: Matthew 10:29, Luke 15:8-10, Galatians 3:5

Stepping Stone: Luke 15:8

> *"Or what woman, having ten silver coins, if she loses one coin, does not light a lamp, sweep the house, and search carefully until she finds it?"*

Believe-it-or-not stories remind me that miracles still happen. One of my favorites comes from my sister, Laurie. Diamonds may not have been this girl's *best friend*, but she treasured her beautiful wedding ring set, the sparkling symbol of her marriage vows.

As a farmer's wife, the daily chores she tackled took her to the barn and all over the property, not to mention a mountain of cooking for farmhands and family. One day, Laurie happened to glance down at her hand and noticed the large diamond in her engagement ring missing. Day after day she swept corners and sifted dustpans of dirt. The tiniest glitter could not escape her scrutiny.

Weeks of feeling like a dirt inspector went by as Laurie searched for her diamond. Any day, a psychiatrist would surely label her compulsive-obsessive. Finally she decided, *No more. It's time I regain my sanity.*

Sure enough, one morning the inevitable happened—*again.* Laurie noticed a speck on the floor that glimmered in the morning sunlight. She wasn't about to take the bait this time—*well, maybe just once more.*

She again sifted through dirt. *Eureka!* She found it! One crusty clod held one dusty diamond in its clutches. Happy tears melted into wonder as she realized how many acres this dirt clod had possibly traveled clinging to the tread of her husband's work boot. How many times had she herded cows and cleaned barns with her diamond perhaps riding along?

Dirt clods and diamonds. The stuff of miracles.

Prayer Pathway: *When I'm ready to give up, I'm so glad that You remain The God of the impossible.*

A Light in the Window

Scripture Trail: Psalm48:1, Psalm 119:105-107, John 8:12

Stepping Stone: John 8:12

> *"Then Jesus spoke to them again saying, 'I am the light of the world. He who follows me shall not walk in darkness, but have the light of life.'"*

"You are going to the hospital." I listened to the doctor's order and swallowed hard. Straight to the point, his words dashed my hopes of a quick fix for my husband's illness.

After much persuasion, Arlen had finally agreed to see our doctor. His *quick fix* turned into a three-day hospital stay. I looked at my strapping man lying in a hospital bed, hooked up to IV and oxygen tubing. Tears threatened to foil my efforts to encourage him.

Since shortly after getting sick, Arlen slept as best he could while sitting up in a recliner. As his coughing increased and his breathing worsened, sleep proved hit and miss for both of us. Despite weariness, I strived to meet his needs, while taking care of our large family.

On the way home from the hospital late one night, I decided to drive by our church. An evangelist was holding special meetings that week. Late evening services or not, it seemed impossible that anyone would still be there at 10:30 p.m.

As I approached the church, I prayed that I'd find someone still hanging around. My car turned the corner and, there in front of me lights shined through the entry window. In that moment, I felt God's love settle over me like a warm blanket on a frosty night. I knew my church family would embrace me and pray with me.

My fatigue lifted as I realized that God had kept the porch light on—just for me.

Prayer Pathway: *No matter how dark my way, may I remember that You keep your porch light shining bright.*

"A mouse ... in my house?"

Scripture Trail: Proverbs 8:17, Isaiah 30:21, Jeremiah 29:12-14

Stepping Stone: Isaiah 30:21

> *"Your ears shall hear a word behind you, saying,*
> *'This is the way, walk in it, whenever you turn to the*
> *right hand or whenever you turn to the left.'"*

Computer geniuses love to cause trouble. I know, because I married one. Along with Arlen's propensity for bantering in Cyberspeak—a language foreign to most of us *normal* folks, he also loves practical jokes. Several years ago, one of his fellow computer geeks loaned him a little black box. An intermittent squeaking noise, much like what a mouse makes, emanated from its innards.

Arlen carefully hid this phony menace inside our couch. For days, evolving into weeks, I searched for *the mouse in my house,* much to my troublemaker's amusement. Just as I thought I knew where the pesky critter was, the noise stopped. I then quietly listened for the squeak to sound again, but with other demands on my time, my patience fizzled fast. *Oh well, he'll show his pointy little face soon enough and then I'll git 'em.* Hours passed between squeaks. Other times the irritating noise sounded just minutes apart.

Fortunately for Arlen, I have a sense of humor—although he admits he pushes his good fortune to the limit. In this case, he even pretended to help me look for his incognito rodent friend. Eventually, my mischievous man fessed up and took his well-deserved lumps.

I've found that life comes with aggravating annoyances that seem to come from nowhere. How often I get in a dither over what I later discover pointless. When I see myself wasting time on senseless distractions, maybe I would do better to move on, trusting God to deal with the source.

Prayer Pathway: *May I shed irritations like water off a duck's*
back, instead of drowning in frustration.

Genius at Work

Scripture Trail: Genesis 1:31, Isaiah 43:19, Romans 9:20-21

Stepping Stone: Genesis 1:31

> *"Then God saw everything that He had made, and indeed it was very good ..."*

Professionals have one thing in common. No matter their expertise, they start out as amateurs. The beginner status carries with it a propensity for error.

'Bumble fingers' describes my initial wall papering adventures. A little catch called *repeating patterns* provides fodder for a bungling novice like me. One of my more famous bloopers happened when I wallpapered my sons' bedroom. I used a pattern with lions and tigers and ... *Oh, my!* Sorry, no bears. But, with wild abandon, elephants, zebras, and giraffes joined in the *zooy* pattern.

Even now I blush over my ridiculous decorating debacle. At the seams, an elephant's head rested on a giraffe's neck. A tiger tried to trade stripes with a zebra. A lion might be king, but his head doesn't fit on an elephant's body.

I'm big time grateful for another product for decorating walls. Back in the era of the seventies when this fiasco happened, strips of burnt cork graced the walls of many a home. A glue gun, and a few floor-to-ceiling 'bars' of this face-saving stuff, covered a multitude of my snafus.

I sighed with relief when I stepped back and saw that the animals no longer looked disjointed as they peered out at me from their wall-to-wall *cage*. The mismatched seams disappeared behind the celebrated cork.

Now, uh ... of course ... umm ... I ... uh ... planned from the beginning for this touch of genius. Maybe it's time I turn in my glue gun.

Prayer Pathway: *With all my ineptitude, God, I need You to cover my mistakes, whether big or small.*

Over-the-top Days

Scripture Trail: Matthew 14:25-32, Philippians 4:13, 1 Peter 4:12

Stepping Stone: Philippians 4:13

> *"I can do all things through Christ who strengthens me."*

At the end of some days, I wish I'd stayed in bed, pulled the covers over my head, and sucked my thumb. A rough time line follows, beginning with leaving my driveway one morning. Read it and weep:

10:30 – Left my house; turned wrong way (my first clue)

11:00 – Dropped son #1 at park and met a friend for coffee

11:45 – Missed son's call for ride home

12:35 – Picked up missed call from stranded son #1

1:20 – Arrived late for Spanish class

3:00 – Son #2 calls; his car broken down on freeway; bought water hose for his car

3:45 – Daughter, with seven young children in her car calls; lost ignition key, at the beach (two hours from home)

4:30 – Back to son #2's overheated car; discovered hose didn't fix problem when engine catches on fire

6:15 – Called tow truck driver for son; left son parked by freeway to wait for driver

7:00 – Drove home for extra car key for daughter; Oops! Hubby has key. Made one-hour round trip to get said key

8:20 – Met relatives to give them car key to rescue daughter

8:40 – Went to pick up son #2 at auto repair shop

9:00 – Son forgets to leave his car key for mechanic; drove back to shop with key

9:20 – Pulled into driveway. Cut arm on car door. OUCH!

Let's see ... God *did* say He would never allow any more than I can handle. I guess I'd better let Him keep His hands on the 'handle' part.

Prayer Pathway: *Lord, when life overwhelms me...please hear my eloquent prayer: "Help!"*

Called To Comfort

Scripture Trail: Isaiah 51:12, Luke 6:31, 2 Corinthians 1:3-5

Stepping Stone: 2 Corinthians 3:4

> *"... that we may be able to comfort those who are in any trouble with the comfort with which we ourselves are comforted by God."*

Let's see. Hmmm ... pick up phone ... dial hospital ... say a cheery, "How ya' doin'?" Wait for a response ... say some uplifting words ... listen as my friend Lorraine weeps, who just lost part of her foot, while I think about what I can say next to comfort her.

Well, "How are you doing yourself?" Her delighted tone caught me off guard.

"Umm ... uh ... Okay, I guess." *Now wait just a minute! Whose idea was this phone call anyway?* I'd planned to pass Lorraine the tissue box through the phone line. Instead she wiped away my tears of concern. Comfort given ... comfort received.

In the cobwebs of my memory bank I remember something about "axioms" in mathematics. My trusty computer dictionary tells me that an axiom may be defined as, "A self-evident or universally recognized truth; a maxim: 'It is an economic axiom as old as the hills that goods and services can be paid for only with goods and services' (Albert Jay Nock)."

I wonder if Mr. Nock was really an incognito Bible scholar disguised as a word nerd? No disrespect intended toward Mr. Nock. His definition seems mighty close to the Apostle Paul's axiom for giving and receiving.

Pass the tissue box of *goods* and offer the *service* of love; without thinking about it, my friend and I received mutual comfort.

Offer comfort. Receive comfort. Amazing how that works ... an axiom as old as the Corinthian hills.

Prayer Pathway: *Even when I'm suffering, help me to give as well as to receive comfort.*

When troubles come, how may I fully rely upon God?

_____

_____

_____

_____

_____

_____

_____

_____

_____

_____

_____

_____

_____

_____

_____

I lay every burden and joy at the feet of Jesus.

"My
fatigue
lifted as I
realized that
God had kept the
porch light on
—just for
me."

Along the Way

When my hands grow weary
In fulfilling my call
God sends His servants along the way

When my heart feels heavy
From loss and grief
God sends His Spirit along the way

When I doubt God can use me
My failures assail me
God sends His Word along the way

When life overwhelms me
All hope eludes me
God sends His Son along the way

Dedicated to The Lover of my Soul

On Holy Ground

Steps

Holy Retail

The Stroke of a Pen

Misbehaving

They Never Knew

Beautiful Dirt

Why Worry Lane

Pollution in Paradise

Just Because

Fire by Night

When Words Aren't Enough

A Holy Embrace

Words on the Wind
Poem

"Then the LORD said to him, 'Take your sandals off your feet, for the place where you stand is holy ground.'"
Acts 7:33

Holy Retail

Scripture Trail: Isaiah 12:2, Jeremiah 29:12-13, John 8:36

Stepping Stone: John 8:36

> *"Therefore if the Son makes you free, you shall be free indeed."*

The Christian bookstore where I worked sat next to a beautiful ice skating rink. People of all ages and backgrounds spent hours on the ice.

While no one would likely blink at the variety of people who showed up at the rink, many might express surprise at the unexpected shoppers who walked through the doors of the Christian book store next door. Predictably, many Christians came looking for gift items, or the latest novel, Bible study, Christian CD, or movie.

However, another group of special customers also frequented the store. As I walked over to a middle-aged woman one day, I noticed her swiping at tears. "I just came from the doctor's office. I'm having a lung biopsy on Monday. I'm not a very religious person, but do you have something I could read that will help me get through this?"

A gray-haired woman shared: "A couple of my kids are having marriage troubles. I don't go to church anywhere, but you got something they could read?"

One day, a man who appeared intoxicated stopped by to shop. His words slurred. "My girl friend's got *can-shur*. I don't know what *tuh* say to her. Could you *h-help* me?"

A young woman scanned the rows of Bibles. She didn't know that there is a New Testament and an Old Testament.

So shoppers come to a *retail* store where followers of Christ *retell* the story of The One who keeps His "Open" sign posted—day and night.

Prayer Pathway: *Jesus, I want to always be ready to lead people to You, The One who has all the answers.*

The Stroke of a Pen

Scripture Trail: Psalm 45:1, Isaiah 40:28, Matthew 5:14-16

Stepping Stone: Psalm 45:1

> *"My heart is overflowing with a good theme ... my tongue is the pen of a ready writer."*

Flaming red and orange hues emblazon an evening sky. Bleary-eyed executives threaten to toss their malfunctioning computer out the nearest office window. Monkeys chatter in staccato bursts while leaping in wide arcs, grasping first one sagging tree branch and then another. Stacie hops aboard her first school bus; Mama cries.

Words from a writer's pen create visual images just as surely as lines and shapes emerge from an artist's brush to reveal stunning portraits. My family laughs at my artistic stick-figure drawings, Even though I may feel rather smug about my talent for penciling stick-people, even I must admit my artwork does not reflect the finer nuances seen in Michelangelo's Sistine Chapel paintings. Nevertheless, my grandchildren love my artsy efforts, often pleading, "Draw it again, Grandma!"

So here I sit attempting to convey my thoughts in words—to paint a word-picture on the canvas of a reader's imagination. I picture God's joy as He breathed life into Adam.

Did The Creator gasp at the inaugural flight of a delicate butterfly as it lit on a crimson rose kissed by dewdrops? Did He laugh at the first barking baby seal? Where does a rainbow really begin and end?

The Master Artist, The Author of all that was, and ever will be, graciously offers the results of His creativity for His children's pleasure. When I leave this earthly life, I long for my limited human skills to one day explode in exquisite expressions of love to my Daddy God.

Prayer Pathway: *Father, will you please take my human talents and use them to bless You?*

Misbehaving

Scripture Trail: Proverbs 22:1, Ecclesiastes 7:1, Isaiah 56:5-7

Stepping Stone: Proverbs 22:1

> *"A good name is to be chosen rather than great riches, loving favor rather than silver and gold."*

Since childhood I've behaved myself in church. That is until one Sunday, when …

The service began as usual with announcements and a few songs. Just before the sermon, the pastor led a quiet time of prayer for the missionaries, directing the congregation to names and faces printed on a bulletin insert.

Distinguished men in suits and ties gazed at the camera. As I focused for a moment on the photos—without warning—*I saw it.*

This was not my fault. Honest … I'm a good girl in church … honest, I am. Enough excuses. Below the bottom edge of a picture, the name of a silver-haired missionary jumped out at me:

Ronald McDonald.

That morning, I sat in front of two older ladies, their demeanor a role model for appropriate church decorum. *Then there was me.* I pursed my lips, as I struggled to stifle a fit of laughter. *Where's a bag to put over my head, when I need one?*

I got up, tiptoed to the restroom, and washed my face with cold water. *Get a grip, Nora.* A few minutes later I returned to my seat, only to lose control again. By this time, I'm sure the nice ladies wanted to stuff one of their lace-edged hankies in my mouth. Maybe they should have. The shock might have helped me settle down.

God understands my reverence for Him. Maybe He snickered just a little too when some mama picked her little Ronnie's name.

Prayer Pathway: *Thank You for loving me, even when what's on the outside doesn't match what's on the inside.*

They Never Knew

Scripture Trail: Matthew 5:16, 1 Timothy 5:17, Titus 2:1-8

Stepping Stone: 1Timothy 5:17

> *"Let the elders who rule well be counted worthy of double honor ..."*

I was a child—she was a woman in her thirties, with a handful of kids. I was a child—he, a gray-haired man. I was a child—she, the wife of a successful executive. Three people profoundly touched my life, never knowing what they had done.

Along with her tribe of children, Jeanette took this half-pint farm girl to the big city. Thousands of Christmas lights glittered in grand displays, thrilling me with my first-time trip to a big shopping mall. She never knew the amazement I felt when she invited me to come along.

Dean simply knelt every time he prayed. He so revered His Lord that he felt compelled to kneel in the presence of his Savior. No big show. No attention desired. He never knew I watched him, much less that 50 years later, I still treasure his godly example.

My young eyes beheld the poise and success reflected in Lu's life. Her words were few and softly spoken. As an enthusiastic teen I promised to show up every day to help in classrooms for our two-week Vacation Bible School. On commencement night she hugged me and said, "You kept your promise." She didn't know the depth of affirmation she imparted to me in that short statement.

God exalts those who walk in humility. Giving honor to whom honor is due, I offer them this sincere tribute.

Belonging. Reverence. Affirmation. Three role models blessed me in lasting measure ... and they never knew.

Prayer Pathway: *May I always remember that what I do impacts others for eternity.*

Beautiful Dirt

Scripture Trail: Genesis 2:7, 18-19, 2 Chronicles 26:10

Stepping Stone: 2 Chronicles 26:10

> *"... he had much livestock, both in the lowlands and in the plains; he also had farmers and vinedressers in the mountains and in Carmel, for he loved the soil."*

Reasons for joy and excitement come in lots of packages. Making no two people alike, God employs endless options in expressing His love to His children. Breathtaking sunsets, rippling streams, and starry nights have inspired many a sonnet.

My niece once phoned me to share an odd source of delight—dirt. Rhonda rejoiced over having dirt dumped at her doorstep. People pay big bucks for dirt when someone provides the labor. But this soil came free of charge, special delivery. One day, she arrived home from running errands to find her hard-working husband, David, spreading dirt for a brick foundation. They were one step closer to building an outdoor art studio in their back yard. Beautiful dirt—the beginning of something wonderful!

As the driver of Mom's Taxi Service, I spent five school years driving a son cross-country to school. The daily half-hour trips to and from the campus gave me lots of time for motherly chats. In the springtime, I raved over the fresh-turned soil in the fields we passed. I exclaimed, "Bobby, look at that beautiful dirt! Isn't it awesome!"

Rolling his eyes, he responded, "Yeah, sure. Whatever." My passenger then leaned his head back for a few more minutes of shuteye. So much for Dirt Appreciation 101.

Even God got His holy hands into dirt. When He finished making man and the animals from out of the ground, He stepped back, looked at His handiwork and said, "This is very good!"

"Ah, dirt ... beautiful dirt."

Prayer Pathway: *Father, may I recognize all Your gifts to me, even when they come 'dirt simple'.*

Why Worry Lane

Scripture Trail: Psalm 94:17-19, Isaiah 26:3, Matthew 6:34

Stepping Stone: Matthew 6:34

> *"You will keep him in perfect peace, whose mind is stayed on You, because he trusts in You."*

My sister, Patty, once lived on a street called Why Worry Lane. Since then, many address changes have happened for her and for me. I still chuckle when I remember the green street sign. I'd like to plunk that sign on my current street corner. The apt reminder would serve me well.

Shortly after Patty moved to Why Worry Lane, Arlen and I moved to Circle Drive in Circle Pines, Minnesota. When I wrote home, I jested about going in circles. How well this describes me. Too many irons in the fire and my fingers in too many pies keep me on a treadmill of busyness.

I often feel like I can't run fast enough, or worse yet, that I am headed even faster to some nebulous place called *Nowhere*. Sound familiar? Doesn't have much to offer, does it?

God enjoys reminding me that He controls the universe; that includes managing my world. I've seen bookmarks, magnets and plaques with the words, "Good morning. This is God. I will be handling all your problems. So have a nice day!" *What a concept.*

Even the Stepping Stone scripture for this devotional nudges me to remember that God minds the store quite well, *without my help.* As I rest in God, He delights in calming me in the midst of life's demands.

Each day I must choose the address where I will reside. Will I stay at my Father's mansion on Why Worry Lane or the enemy's Anxiety Inn on Circle Drive?

Prayer Pathway: *Lord, instead of worrying and going in circles, may I head straight to You for direction.*

Pollution in Paradise

Scripture Trail: Psalm 107:29, Isaiah 26: 1-3, John 14:27

Stepping Stone: John 14:27

> *"Peace I leave with you, My peace I give to you; not as the world gives do I give to you. Let not your heart be troubled, neither let it be afraid."*

Arlen and I stood on the empty land where we would soon build a new house. The treed lot resembled a natural park, placed in the middle of a suburban neighborhood. We looked at a stream meandering across the back of the property, marveling at our corner of paradise.

Our excitement bubbled over as we invited our friends, David and Melba, to walk the land with us. We could hear birds chatter while the water rippled over rocks and twigs. A light wind whispered through the tall evergreens. I asked everyone to be quiet just for a couple minutes so we could all soak in the peaceful surroundings. "Listen. Hear how quiet it is?" I enthused.

Crash! Bam! Crunch! I jumped when the clamor of a car accident not far away demolished the serene moment. Just as though a dozen garbage trucks had driven up and dumped their loads of junk on our property, noise pollution assaulted our senses. Sirens from police cars and emergency vehicles added their part in shattering the stillness.

Time to refocus. We stood in our wooded haven, safe and healthy, while others dealt with possible injury or even death. Noise invaded our silence, while pain and fear likely devastated their world. Was the grass still green under our feet? *Yes.* Did the birds still sing around us? *Yes.*

In blessing and in pain, God reminds me that He remains near in every circumstance ... for all ... and for always.

Prayer Pathway: *Jesus, in the midst of blessing, may I be quick to pray when I know people are hurting.*

Just Because

Scripture Trail: Jeremiah 31:3, Romans 12:10, 1 Peter 1:22

Stepping Stone: 1 Peter 1:22

> *"Since you have purified your souls in obeying the truth through the Spirit in sincere love for the brethren, love one another fervently with a pure heart."*

When least expected, *just because* moments sneak up on me Moments of blessing, words of love, and treasures of kindness have filled my life with joy more than any material riches.

I'm having a *just because* moment today. Arlen loves me, even through my meltdowns. My daughter, Tyana, has a knack for calling me when I most need a boost. My daughter-in-law, Kali, regularly cooks a meal for Mom and Dad, much to our tummies' delight. Gail, my friend since junior high, lights up my world when we hang out. Chatting with my friends from church always lifts my spirits.

Loving family members, friends, and church family, too numerous to name them all, but so appreciated, have stood by me through long-term chronic illness. So many loved ones have helped me, making life not only doable, but sweet.

My grown up kids and their families planned a "Pajama Grandma" party for my 61st birthday. With illness keeping me in my jammies, **everyone**—even the macho guys—wore their PJs just to make me laugh. Another incredible daughter-in-law, Jennifer, even led the clan in a *Pajama Grandma* song and dance.

As months have turned into years, loved ones continue praying daily for my health needs. So many thoughtful people have blessed me that I wish I could emboss each person's name in gold on a scroll stretched across the sky.

In this quiet moment, I see the faces of numerous relatives and friends and gratitude overwhelms me … *just because.*

Prayer Pathway: *Father, I'm humbled that You love me deeply— just because.*

Fire by Night

Scripture Trail: Exodus 40:36-39, Psalm 19:1, Psalm 31:3

Stepping Stone: Psalm 31:3

> *"You are my rock and my fortress; therefore, for Your name's sake lead me and guide me."*

"Sunrise … sunset. Sunrise … sunset." Feels like a song coming on. Frequently I pause in whatever I'm doing and watch the horizon, as God fashions vivid colors in breathtaking patterns. What magnificent paintings He splashes across the heavens.

One evening, while driving to a friend's home at dusk, I noticed neon pinks and oranges in the distance. At the end of this day, I marveled at God's day-ending encore. To my amazement, a design emerged unlike anything I'd ever seen. Instead of neon wisps of clouds, a massive pink column appeared, similar to a giant pillar stretching vertically downward from heaven to touch the earth.

At first, my mind couldn't accept what my eyes saw. The pillar of bright colors shone so distinctly … so perfectly … so uniquely, I did a triple take. Immediately I thought of the Israelites following a pillar of fire by night.

Scripture sums up my reaction to God's twilight display. *"The heavens declare the glory of God; the firmament shows His handiwork."* This beautiful verse from Psalm 19:1 reminds me that God still demonstrates His presence. He is real. He is available. He is in control.

On that stunning sunset evening, I felt God's earnest desire to assure me … not just any "me" … *but me*—Nora Peacock—that His guiding hand and His pillar of fire rests over me. He does not leave me or forsake me. My anxieties fade in the face of His glory sent to earth.

Prayer Pathway: *God, I'm so grateful that You still reveal Yourself in miraculous ways.*

When Words Aren't Enough

Scripture Trail: Psalm 95:6, 1 Timothy 4:13-15, 1 Peter 1:8

Stepping Stone: Psalm 95:6

> *"Oh come, let us worship and bow down; let us kneel before the LORD our Maker."*

The dust has settled after attending one more writer's conference. Without hesitation, I express my gratitude to Oregon Christian Writers that just celebrated 50 years of helping writers to pursue excellence.

Once again, for four summer days, I soaked up knowledge provided by skilled teachers. Workshops included subjects such as editing, novel writing, public speaking, storyboarding, crafting poetry, as well as delving into e-books and blogging. Scientists say humans use only a small fraction of their brain capacity, but my noggin' begs to differ after a week of cramming abundant information into every crevice and corner of the gray matter that lies between my ears.

Unlike the dog-eat-dog business world, I've experienced first-hand the nurturing spirit that pours forth from OCW speakers, teachers, and conferees. Whether beginners or advanced level, writers learn to fan into flame the gifting and passion God has given them. One OCW newbie, Cara Grandle, signed a contract with a successful and highly respected agent. Fellow novelists rejoiced for Cara, a first-timer to a writer's conference. Competitive attitudes took no place.

But more exciting than the learning opportunities—than all the success stories, I basked in the presence of Holy God—the Author of my faith. The memories still bring sweet tears. As I meditate on my encounter with The Giver of all that is good, I struggle to wrap words around the 'inexpressible'.

And so I take a deep breath because He knows my every thought—even when words aren't enough.

Prayer Pathway: *Lord, how I love You. When words fail me, thank You for filling in the blanks.*

A Holy Embrace

Scripture Trail: Matthew 18:5, Mark 9:37, Luke 9:48

Stepping Stone: Matthew 18:5

> *"Whoever receives one little child like this in My name receives Me."*

It was love at first sight. Her *I-know-something-you-don't-know* smile drew me to her. We connected on a level that I still don't fully understand.

I don't recall her name. She wouldn't mind. She came from out of town with her mother to visit our church—only once. We sat next to each other for several minutes.

After a while she climbed into my lap and, for half an hour, she rested her head on my shoulder. I held her as I marveled at the gift of trust she extended to me.

I wept as I felt Jesus' arms wrap around the two of us. He embraced us as one—our hearts were so intimately knit. His presence felt tangible.

My newfound friend was 15—going on 2. Her physical features were typical of a child with Down syndrome. People may claim such children are a mistake. They might question her value. What could she possibly contribute to this world?

One may agonize over the theological 'whys' of children born with disabling defects that last their lifetime. That day I didn't go down that road. Neither did she. Instead, we shared a holy moment.

I seldom experience moments so sacred I can scarcely breathe. Preachers who share their passionate messages bless me. Missionary stories of sacrifice make me cry. But even these servants must take a back seat to a young girl who stopped time for me to sit with her—and Jesus. I will never be the same.

Prayer Pathway: *Divine Creator, how good to know that You made no mistake in creating a single one of us.*

Lord, in this holy moment, I take off my shoes and offer You these words of praise:

I lay every burden and joy at the feet of Jesus.

"My
anxieties
fade in the face of
His glory
sent to
earth."

Words on the Wind

Elusive words—longing for expression
Flooding my heart, filling my mind
Take flight, oh words of love
On the wind of The Spirit
To the arms of my Savior
For this child cannot contain you

Elusive words—longing for expression
Guiding my days, guarding my nights
Take flight, oh words of thanks
On the wind of The Spirit
To the heart of my Savior
For this child cannot contain you

Elusive words—longing for expression
Redeeming my life, restoring my soul
Take flight, oh words of praise
On the wind of The Spirit
To the feet of my Savior
For this child cannot contain you

This child cannot contain you

Dedicated to my
New Life Church family
In my time of greatest need,
you were there.

Resting in Him

Steps

Watching Over Me

Sleeping on the Job

Recharging My Battery

Heaven's Quiet Corner

Nesting

The Eye of the Storm

Stepping Off the Fast Track

The State of Contentment

Sweet Dreams

"Relaxed … really?"

Be Still My Soul

Sounds of Silence
Poem

*"Come to Me, all you who labor and
are heavy laden, and I will give you rest."
Matthew 11:28*

Watching Over Me

Scripture Trail: Psalm 127: 2-3, Psalm 138:8, Proverbs 3:24

Stepping Stone: Psalm 127:2

> *"It is vain for you to rise up early, to sit up late, to eat the bread of sorrows, for so He gives His beloved sleep."*

As I write this devotional the clock shows 3:47, as in *0-dark thirty*. Waking up in the middle of the night is not uncommon for me. Growing older goes hand-in-hand with late night tea parties for one. If only I could blame aging for my restlessness.

Sometimes my eyes refuse to close and I use the opportunity for quiet moments with God—no phones ringing, no demands from anyone. Other times I'm awake because I feel troubled … like tonight, for example.

God faithfully reminds me that He stays awake 24-7. His gentle correction comforts me when I read, *"It is vain to rise up early, to sit up late, to eat the bread of sorrows."*

I hurt tonight for a child I dearly love. I expect I'm not alone as a parent or grandparent who burns the midnight oil over a troubled youngster. Although my love runs deep, how vain to sit up worrying as though my anxiety will fix anything. God loves my children and grandchildren far more than I do. He remains well able to *"perfect that which concerns me." (Psalm 138:8)*

My heavenly Father tells me I am His beloved; He offers me hope and rest. Time to go lie down and let my Abba Father pull the blanket of His love up over me.

I think I hear Him whispering in my ear, "Sweet dreams, Nora." How reassuring to know that, while I sleep, my Father God watches over me and mine.

Prayer Pathway: *May I find restoring rest that comes from knowing You always stay on duty.*

Sleeping on the Job

Scripture Trail: Leviticus 26:4-6, Psalm 4:8, Jeremiah 31:26

Stepping Stone: Psalm 4:8

> *"I will both lie down in peace, and sleep; for You alone, O LORD, make me dwell in safety."*

Church camp. There's nothing like those weeks of summer fun and fond memories.

My young eyes danced with laughter at the old woman in tennis shoes, who wore a baseball cap backwards, while standing on top of the piano to give announcements. After all, Miss Jean had to be at least 50 years old!

I was among the privileged age group who got to spend the last girlie night of camp under the stars. Between adolescent bouts of giggles, we rolled out sleeping bags and nestled down for a few winks. Our fearless leader held no claim to such youthfulness and soon fell fast asleep, serenading us with her sonorous snoring.

Some wet blanket once said that all good things must come to an end. In our case, our blankets did indeed get wet when a jarring storm crashed the party. Thunder rumbled and Miss Jean slept. Lightning lit up the sky and Miss Jean still slept. As the downpour increased, we shrieked and ran back to our cabins … and Miss Jean? She did the impossible and slumbered on through wind … and rain … thunder … and screaming girls.

I've often wished for an instant replay of that soggy night. Oh, what I would give to have a picture of Miss Jean's panic-stricken face when she awakened to clear morning skies and ALL her campers nowhere in sight. One *old woman* captured the hearts and imaginations of the young—and all the while she slept like a baby.

Prayer Pathway: *When storms surround me, may others see Your peace in my life and say, "I want that!"*

Recharging My Battery

Scripture Trail: Psalm 18:1-2, Isaiah 25:9, Acts 1:8

Stepping Stone: Isaiah 25:9

> *"... Behold, this is our God; we have waited for Him, and He will save us ... we will be glad and rejoice in His salvation."*

My car sits in my driveway tonight, deader than a mackerel in the desert. All set to head for a friend's house, I tossed my stuff in the car just in time to join rush hour traffic. Then I slid behind the wheel, inserted the key and ... nothing. Zippo. Nada. The engine didn't even have the decency to groan and sputter.

I cranked the starter again and held my tongue just the right way. I even bit my lower lip and then spoke firmly to my rebellious chariot. The darkened panel of gauges mocked my efforts.

Were I a man, I would have gotten out, lifted the hood, and surveyed the wires, hoses, and whatchamacallits on the engine. I might have even looked at the black box with the positive and negative thingies, but a lot of good that would've done without another vehicle to give me a jumpstart.

So there my car sits in my driveway until my knight in shining armor comes home.

Now that I've had a couple of hours to simmer down, I count my blessings. I'm not stranded at the side of some freeway while thousands of cars swoosh past me, leaving me in peril of my life. No hot sun baking me or frost numbing my hands. I'm not at the mercy of a stranger who might or might not come with the best intentions.

Poor me. I now sit in my comfortable house with unexpected time to write. Life is hard.

Prayer Pathway: *When problems drain my energy and emotions, please jumpstart my weary heart.*

Heaven's Quiet Corner

Scripture Trail: Psalm 23:1-3, Hebrews 4:9, Revelation 8:1

Stepping Stone: Revelation 8:1

> *"When He opened the seventh seal, there was silence in heaven for about half an hour."*

Lots of kids equal lots of noise. This proven mathematical formula supports the theory of relativity: namely, the noise factor is *greater than or equal to* the number of *relatives* (i.e. kids) in a house. A fractional way to represent this formula follows:

$$\text{Noise} = \frac{\text{\# of Kids}}{\text{House}} \quad \text{or} \quad N = \frac{K}{H}$$

The above equation has great bearing on my aversion to noise. Many children later, including a season with five teenagers at once, left me with glazed eyes at the end of each day.

To my amazement, the day finally arrived when my youngest child started school and I rediscovered sweet silence. Bless their darlin' little britches, my kids worried about poor Mom pining away with loneliness.

When my kiddos asked me what I did when the house was empty, I should have answered, "Why, I keep myself busy being a *Proverbs 31 Woman*!" But that would have zoomed right over their tousled heads.

Satisfaction, with a healthy dash of smugness, welled up within me. I let my cherubs know that I turned off everything. No television. No dryer with tennis shoes thudding. No dishwasher rattling plates and pans—*no nothin'*. I basked in precious moments of soothing silence.

My children just knew that Mom had *lost it*. Their standard-issue response to my joy? "How boring!"

God put one special verse in the Bible for frazzled moms like me: *"there was silence in heaven for about half an hour."* Yep, I'm hanging my potholders on that one.

Prayer Pathway: *Just so I don't forget to say it, "Thanks God, for every single quiet moment You give me!"*

Nesting

Scripture Trail: Deuteronomy 32:10-12, Psalm 84:3, Hebrews 4:9

Stepping Stone: Psalm 84:3

> *"Even the sparrow has found a home, and the swallow a nest for herself, where she may lay her young ..."*

Papa and Mama Robin have decided to build their new home right outside my living room window. They've cruised the neighborhood, checked out the available real estate, and chosen the fork in a tree next to our house. Maybe they knew the Peacock family, fellow birds of a feather, would appreciate them.

After the excitement and busyness of numerous trips to construct their homey nest, Mr. and Mrs. Robin face the tedious part. While I eagerly wait to see if twins, triplets, or even quadruplets are on the way, Mama Robin warms her incubating young'uns. Day after day, she sits.

Papa Robin shows up from time to time and chirps his needs at his wife. "Let's go have some fun!" Mama still sits. Papa persists. "Ah, come on ... they'll be okay for a few minutes. All work and no play makes for a dull bird!" In the interest of marital harmony, she listens to her mate and reluctantly leaves her babes.

Mama Robin tore herself away from her precious eggs and Papa Robin proved right. She returned to find them still safe in their nest. As I've watched my feathered friends, Mrs. Robin has shown me that she can leave her chicks so she may have fun with Mr. Robin—and it's okay.

Maybe I'll take a housewarming gift to Mrs. Robin. I wonder if she would enjoy a dirt cake, complete with Gummy Worms. Then I'll fly off on a country drive with Mr. Peacock. *What a concept.*

Prayer Pathway: *Lord, help me to gladly set aside time to nest, to rest, and to have fun with my loved ones.*

The Eye of the Storm

Scripture Trail: Psalm 89:8-9, Psalm 93:4, Mark 4:39

Stepping Stone: Psalm 89:9

> *"You rule the raging of the sea; when its waves rise, You still them."*

When my family gathers for holiday dinners we number about 40 people. Relatives sit wherever they can find a spot, often on the floor with their dinner plate in their lap. No worries. We're all good at stepping between legs and slipping around backs. No one complains about the crowding. Unwilling to have anyone stay away, everyone rolls with the space challenges.

Large families provide opportunities for lots of fun, as well as multiple crises. While enjoying a cozy evening with Arlen, the thought hit me: *At this moment, all is quiet on the home front.*

I went down my mental checklist. This son, this daughter, this relative, and that relative were doing well. No obvious problems loomed large on the horizon. No fires to put out. Not one doctor appointment scheduled on my calendar. Our bills were paid. The sky wasn't about to drop on my head.

I smiled at Arlen and said, "It feels like we're in the eye of the storm. I wonder how long this will last." *Silly me.* I held high hopes for a week, or even two, of smooth sailing. *I could get used to this ... I really could.*

But just hours after my cheerful soliloquy, one of our kiddos called in crisis. That's all it took for me to pile out of my mental hammock. Mama to the rescue!

*The eye of the storm ... m*aybe I should hang out there, even when winds of worry roar all around me.

Prayer Pathway: *When the winds of life's storms batter me, help me trust in You, Lord.*

Stepping Off the Fast Track

Scripture Trail: Genesis 13:17, Psalm 55:14, Psalm 116:5-9

Stepping Stone: Psalm 55:14

> *"We took sweet counsel together, and walked to the house of God …"*

Arlen enjoys teasing me about taking my *annual walk*. An athlete I am not. Occasionally, I give in to my conscience and do what I know I should do, but avoid whenever possible—exercise. It's really not that bad, but oh, how I struggle to get myself in gear.

This evening I walked with my son around our neighborhood. The sunny weather and light breeze made an excursion outside irresistible. Walking becomes even more appealing when my husband or one of my kids asks me to go with them.

Besides pleasant companionship, walking has another benefit. For someone like me, who thinks she has to always hurry through life, I must slow down. As I stroll, I see beauty that I overlook when I'm rushing around in my car to get somewhere *yesterday*.

Tonight I noticed, for the first time, a refreshing waterfall in a neighbor's yard. A child successfully maneuvered his bike with training wheels on a short solo trip. And a clever green bug landed on my son's shorts for a free ride.

Sometimes I wonder what I miss by living on the fast track. After taking this tour on foot, I believe I miss a lot. When driving, I focus on *avoiding* instead of *enjoying* the child on the bike. Waterfalls and ingenious bugs miss my notice altogether.

No doubt, that quick-thinking little critter thanked us for our stroll. To his relief, he did not have to fly to his destination without a breather.

Prayer Pathway: *Help me slow down enough to smell the roses along life's pathway.*

The State of Contentment

Scripture Trail: Philippians 4:9-12, 1Timothy 6:6, Hebrews 13:5

Stepping Stone: Philippians 4:11

> *"Not that I speak in regard to need, for I have learned in whatever state I am, to be content."*

With the gray skies that frequent our beautiful state, Oregonians learn to grab every glimpse of sunshine they can. Life's challenges come at me, much like Oregon's persistent rain. When troubles fall in constant showers I need to keep my gaze toward The Son, especially when those showers become monsoons.

Several years ago, a recession slammed Arlen's computer business. Reluctantly, we sold our 3200 square foot dream house on three acres in the country and moved into a much smaller residence. Soon after, with the loss of more business, we landed in a thousand square foot apartment with a postage stamp grassy area.

I learned to live in another state—the State of Contentment. Our first Peacock nest we occupied as newlyweds consisted of 600 square feet. The bathroom came in a quaint size one; not even our young skinny figures could get past each other.

With our double bed pushed against one wall, we fit one dresser in our bedroom giving us a whopping eighteen inches for our feet. "Compact" became the operative word for our honeymoon suite.

Did I miss our big house in the country? Absolutely. But guess what. We were happy campers in our first dinky corner of paradise. Although the latter apartment was much bigger than our newlywed haven, life felt more cramped than cozy. Chalk it up to collecting stuff. However, I do respectfully ask God to keep us in a size two bathroom for our old-married folks' profiles.

Prayer Pathway: *Lord, teach me to remain deep-down content, no matter 'the state' I'm in.*

Sweet Dreams

Scripture Trail: Psalm 126:1-3, Daniel 1:17, Joel 2:28

Stepping Stone: Psalm 126:1

> *"When the LORD brought back the captivity of Zion,
> we were like those who dream."*

"Great is Thy faithfulness! Great is Thy faithfulness! Morning by morning ..." Melodic voices filled my dream, joining in four-part harmony. Just as I warbled along with the next verse, my big toe got stuck in the pages. Yes, my big toe.

I couldn't extricate my foot from under the blankets to flip the next song sheet so that I could continue accompanying my majestic *dream choir*. Whatever would I do if my feet couldn't conduct the next page of music? (I'm still dreaming, folks.)

Finally, I woke up struggling to disentangle my foot from my twisted covers. Even as I laughed at myself, this beautiful song hovered in my thoughts. How I love waking memories that put a smile on my face.

I've also had repeated dreams that haven't been so enjoyable. The classic free-falling scenario has entered my dream world many times. The all-important question arises: *Did she wake up before she hit bottom?* Fatalists would predict that doing so would mean the end of me. Well, I'm still here and I believe I landed with a thud a time or two in these dreams.

But if dream I must, I like the visits to dreamland where I rouse from slumber to songs of God's love and faithfulness. *Twinkle Toes* will even sacrifice a twisted-up foot in bed sheets to begin my day serenaded by The Master's music.

But when the not-so-good dreams come, may I free fall into the arms of my Abba Father, Daddy God.

Prayer Pathway: *By day and by night, may my greatest dreams revolve around seeking You, Lord.*

"Relaxed … really?"

Scripture Trail: Psalm 16:9, Psalm 116:7, Hebrews 4:9-10

Stepping Stone: Hebrews 4:10

> *"For he who has entered His rest has himself also ceased from his works as God did from His."*

Confession time. I come before you with faltering lips and admit the following: "My name is Nora and I am a *cardaholic*." So there it is—in writing no less—for the world to see.

I am a woman on a mission when card shopping. Time matters not as I stand before rows of cards. When it comes to over-the-hill birthdays, my motto still stands: "No mercy."

The years of living with my *card disorder* have taken a toll on my husband. Once in a while Arlen decides it's payback time. On one such occasion, he found a card with a cover picture of a worm resting on a rock. Only problem: the worm *rested* stiff as a board. The word "Relax!" written inside delighted my *King of Comebacks*.

Arlen knows me all too well. Even when I rest in my cozy recliner, I mentally tick off a list of *gotta-dos* and *crisis concerns*. I could use a computer with unlimited memory to keep track of my endless lists.

As I age, my mind and body don't have the same energy to expend on my lists. God shows me through His Word, and through experience, the futility of worry.

He does not withhold His peace from me—I forget to embrace the peace He offers. His mercy always remain a prayer away.

Just maybe God has a new slogan for me. "His mercies are new every morning!" *Hmm … I think I'll ponder that one for a spell.*

Prayer Pathway: *Lord, when my 'relax' switch gets stuck, please disconnect my 'worry' wires.*

Be Still My Soul

Scripture Trail: Psalm 42:5, Ecclesiastes 4:6, Isaiah 32:16-18

Stepping Stone: Isaiah 32:18

> *"My people will dwell in a peaceful habitation, in secure dwellings, and in quiet resting places."*

The apartment that was. In spring and summer, lawn mowers and weed whackers buzzed outside the living room window. Long-haul trucks, souped up cars, and motorcycles zoomed down the freeway a block away, causing a steady drone similar to the ocean's roar. When vehicles collided, sirens soon screamed: "Emergency! Clear the way!" Airliners headed to PDX added to the suburban noise.

From inside my home, the floor above me creaked as people walked around upstairs. From the unit next door, an electric guitar whined from a cranked-up sound system. *Where was the manager?* Lacking air-conditioning, whirring fans cooled the small living room.

Wherever I live, noise finds its way into my world. When one sound stops, another takes its place: a microwave, a grass blower, a hammer, a pressure washer, a street sweeper.

In the midst of this assault on my ears, my mind, and my emotions, I hear birds singing. Beautiful songs, orchestrated by God Himself, pierce through the din. When noise surrounds me on every side, God sends His tiny winged creatures. Even above the racket, if I listen closely, I can hear them. They offer their lilting tune, *Peace be still ... peace be still.*

When clamor steals my rest, He speaks, *Peace, my child.* His miniature messengers impart the Holy Spirit's quiet voice. Small enough to nestle in my hand, His tiny sparrows beat back the clatter that comes with living life.

As I tune out the world, His tender Spirit stills my troubled soul.

Prayer Pathway: *No matter how loud the disruptions that surround me, calm my spirit as only You can do.*

The 'hurrier' I go, the 'behinder' I get. How would Jesus change this for me?

_____

_____

_____

_____

_____

_____

_____

_____

_____

_____

_____

_____

_____

_____

I lay every burden and joy at the feet of Jesus.

"But
when the
not-so-good
dreams come,
may I free fall into
the arms of my
Abba Father,
Daddy God."

Sounds of Silence

Cradled on crisp breezes

Lifted on whimsical currents

Spiraling downward—ever downward

Beauty captured in golds and greens

Your secret purpose revealed

Twirling softly—ever softly

A song hidden within you

Your melody floats before me

Singing silently to my grateful heart

"And when he had opened the seventh seal, there was silence in heaven about the space of half an hour."
Revelation 8:1

In special appreciation to The Holy Spirit Who inspired John to write a special promise for shell-shocked moms like me

"If the shoe fits ..."

Steps

"If the shoe fits …"

Listless and Loving Life

"I'm gonna eat worms."

Country Bumpkins

"How's that spelled?"

Ode to an Oxymoron

Say, "Cheese!"

Free to be …

Wearing O' the Green

Spontaneous Combustion

Taking My Medicine

Laughter
Poem

*"Therefore, if the Son makes you free,
you shall be free indeed."
John 8:36*

"If the shoe fits …"

Scripture Trail: Joshua 5:15, Deuteronomy 25:10, Ruth 4:7-8

Stepping Stone: Ruth 4:7

> *"Now this was the custom in former times in Israel … to confirm anything: one man took off his sandal and gave it to the other …"*

While shoes carry me from one place to another, they also do more than just cover my feet. How many times have I heard my sons exclaim how they could run faster and jump higher in their new basketball shoes? When I was a little girl, I felt like a princess in my new shiny patent shoes.

I don't want to count how many pairs of shoes reside in my closet. I simply *must* have tennies to go with my jeans, and black heels to wear for evenings out, and sandals for warm weather, and fuzzy slippers to go with my jammies, and flip flops for the beach. Well a woman can never have too many shoes!

As long as I have on the right pair of shoes for the right occasion, I can enjoy my day with a measure of confidence. But, if I were to arrive at work in my slippers, the world would end. I would have to go back home to change, or better yet—go to the nearest store and add to the stockpile in my closet.

Shoes meant something special in the Bible. When a man made an agreement, he took off a shoe and gave it to the other party, thus sealing the transaction.

The man who gave up his shoe most likely didn't have twenty replacement pairs, and walking home barefoot or limping with one shoe off weren't great options.

New shoes. Maybe I should learn to appreciate the old ones.

Prayer Pathway: *Whether I offer my shoe, a handshake, or sign a contract, may I keep my word.*

Listless and Loving Life

Scripture Trail: Proverbs 7:2-3, Proverbs 8:17, Isaiah 30:8

Stepping Stone: Isaiah 30:8

> *"Now go, write it before them on a tablet, and note it on a scroll that for time to come forever and ever."*

"Making a list and checking it twice." I'm not the jolly fellow in the red suit, but I do like lists. I make a list for just about everything. My husband accuses me of needing a flowchart for my lists.

People say opposites attract. Arlen and I prove that statement true, at least regarding the list issue. He reluctantly uses a list when he has to shop for more than three items. For him, using a list constitutes a desperate self-defense move. Only then will he endure a list, rather than go back to the store for what he forgot to pick up ... which is exactly my point.

Lists = Remembering.

No Lists = Forgetting.

For me, life without lists is like Linus without his blanket. Life without lists threatens my security. For Arlen, life with lists is like tax regulations—annoying and endless. Life without lists liberates him. He goes with the flow, while I still need a flowchart.

So who wins this crucial debate: *to list or not to list?* I must add that question to my list of questions to ask Jesus. When I arrive at The Pearly Gates, I will probably scramble to find where I put my list that notes this burning question, while my hubby sits eagerly listening to Jesus' answers.

In heaven, debates about lists will cease because the *list issue* won't matter. I'll spend eternity asking my questions, while Jesus ticks off every bullet point on my need-to-know agenda.

Prayer Pathway: *Lord, I want to trust You to answer my questions—with or without a list.*

"I'm gonna eat worms."

Scripture Trail: Genesis 2:7, Isaiah 43:19, Isaiah 55:8-9

Stepping Stone: Isaiah 55:8

> *"'My thoughts are not your thoughts, nor are your ways My ways,' says the Lord."*

Most people have a few zany friends in their life. I need such friends to help me lighten up. Years ago, one such mischievous girlfriend taught me the finer points of making goofy cakes.

Judi keeps me guessing what crazy cake she will come up with next. Besides her cactus cake and her hamburger cake, one of my favorites is the dirt cake. She puts multiple layers of crumbled Oreo cookies, chocolate pudding and cream cheese in a flowerpot, then tops it off with an artificial flower sprouting from the 'dirt mix'. Embedded Gummy Worms enhance its flavor. The finishing touch comes when Judi serves the cake with a garden trowel.

I've had great fun making numerous dirt cakes. Both little children and adults sometimes refuse to eat this delicious concoction. When I start *eating dirt* and pull out a juicy worm, their eyes cross. For a few seconds, they can't accept what they see. Even when the *Aha!* comes, the more squeamish observers still can't handle eating what looks like dirt, much less swallow a 'worm'.

Jesus, The Master of the unexpected, turned water into wine, and fed thousands with two fish and five loaves of bread. While these astonishing events carry eternal significance, I wonder if He didn't chuckle at the perplexed expressions on people's faces.

Next time life's hard and I'm tempted to whine, "I'm gonna eat worms," I'm guessing Jesus will have a surprise up His sleeve that may cause me to do a double take.

Prayer Pathway: *When life doesn't make sense, Lord, help me remember that You know exactly what's up.*

Country Bumpkins

Scripture Trail: Proverbs 13:7, Ecclesiastes 5:18, James 2:1-5

Stepping Stone: Proverbs 13:7

> *"There is one who makes himself rich, yet has nothing; and one who makes himself poor, yet has great riches."*

My license for making fun of country bumpkins? *I are one.* Yup. Me and my spouse. That's us—Ma and Pa Kettle.

Blessed with $300 in gift certificates for a ritzy hotel, Arlen and I looked forward to our anniversary getaway. Not totally clueless, we knew we'd have to watch for hidden expenses.

Pa Kettle didn't see the sign: Overnight Parking $25. First mistake. We tipped the attendant who parked our car, then had to tip the guy who pushed the luggage cart to our room, because ... *perish the thought* that we'd push it ourselves. I hope he didn't see me roll my eyes at the thought of my 6'2" husband straining himself to unload our suitcases.

When we arrived in our room, a basket of nuts and candies gave us a warm fuzzy feeling. But I'd gotten smart by now. I glanced around for a price list and didn't see one. *Oh, look what the nice people gave us!* Second mistake: we opened a two-ounce bag of chips and three baby-sized containers of nuts. Then Ma Kettle (as in me) picked up a paper from the floor—the price list. *Gulp!* Twenty-two bucks on junk food that would fit in a zip lock sandwich bag.

Alas! Our pouch of gold nuggets looked mighty low. But not all was lost! A ritzy food court with the ambiance of cascading water fountains saved the day. With our meager remaining funds, us'ns dined right good on fine and fancy vittles.

Prayer Pathway: *Teach me to seek true riches that last.*

"How's that spelled?"

Scripture Trail: Psalm 139:1-4, Daniel 10:12, Hebrews 4:12

Stepping Stone: Psalm 139:4

> *"For there is not a word on my tongue, but behold, O LORD, You know it all together."*

"Roses are red. Violets are blue. Sugar is sweet and __ __ __." Around kindergarten age, children learn to fill in the blanks.

"Jack be nimble. Jack be quick. Jack jump over ___ _____." Grade school kids raise their hands. "Teacher! Teacher! I know! I know!"

Okay. Let's make this harder. "He ain't heavy, he's my _____." Any adults over 40 miss this one?

So far, so good. Here's one last challenge for the ol' noodle. "How do you spell relief? _____." *Roll with me on this one.*

My ever-faithful friend, Sue, took on the daunting task of editing my writing. I had just waxed eloquent about a teenager who always rushes out the door at the last possible second to catch the school bus. His mother came home one day and found the front door ajar and unlocked. My *clever* summation of my character's fuming response: "Lock the door? How's that spelled?"

Without uttering a word, Sue's reaction to my character's sarcasm spoke volumes: *Nora, are you nuts?* When Mom did not find an intruder, to simply write: "Mom sighed with relief," would have sufficed. My literary creativity landed flatter than a balloon run over by a steamroller.

But all was not lost. My famous line that fizzled was not for naught! I've discovered a great weight-loss plan for writers (and unsuspecting editors). Write a dumb line, laugh yourself silly, and lose ten pounds while watching your readers scratch their heads. That works for me!

Prayer Pathway: *Father, thank You for the freedom to be who I am, even when I don't make a lick of sense.*

Ode to an Oxymoron

Scripture Trail: Luke 6:45, 2 Corinthians 4:2, 2 Timothy 2:14-15

Stepping Stone: 2 Timothy 2:15

> *"Be diligent to present yourself approved to God, a worker who does not need to be ashamed, rightly dividing the word of truth."*

The ultimate oxymoron sits chilling in my refrigerator. On a Friday night, after a very long workweek, some frazzled think tank employee (Herbert's a good name) must have surely stepped over the edge when he created the nonsensical label for this product. I suspect his boss told him, "Produce—or else!"

Weight-conscious females around the world owe their peace of mind to Herbie's creativity. If a girl can lose pounds, have her cake, and eat it too ... well, any calorie counter worth her sugar will go for it, of course! *Hmm, I wonder, is that what 'pound' cake means?*

Oh, sorry ... back to the infamous label. Please savor e-v-e-r-y word on this astounding tribute to English language weirdness. Maybe Herbert wrote single words on scraps of paper, threw them up in the air, and then put together whatever landed face up. And to think, his boss probably patted him on the back for his brilliance.

Oh, yes ... and now for the label. Please don't skip over a single part. Imagine taking this clever creation out of your refrigerator. Here it is: FAT-FREE CREAM.

As a farm girl, I recollect where cream comes from. I milked many a cow and there ain't no city slicker merchandiser gonna convince this ol' milk hand that there's cream without fat. But maybe Herbie thinks we gals who yearn to lose inches are desperate enough to swallow his idea whole.

Fat-free or not, it's been fun skimming silliness off the top.

Prayer Pathway: *Though I enjoy playing with words, Lord, may I always wisely handle Your Word.*

Say, "Cheese!"

Scripture Trail: Exodus 35:35, Psalm 90:16-17, Isaiah 65:2

Stepping Stone: Exodus 35:35

> *"He has filled them with skill to do all manner of work of the engraver ... those who do every work and those who design artistic works."*

He leaned over, aiming his camera *just so*. Gliding the lens adjustment a fraction in one direction and then back a tad, he gave a thumbs up. This shoot would be a good one. No fuzzy edges. No double images or unwanted shadows.

From my car I noticed the man sizing up his intended subject from several angles. As I drove closer he bent over, while continuing to fine-tune his camera settings. Surely a person who cared so much about the end product must dream of fame and fortune. Perhaps this would be *the* perfect shot that would land his superb photos in National Geographic.

As I approached the intersection, the traffic light turned red just in time for me to behold the object of the photographer's attention. Could it be a spectacular flower? Perhaps he had discovered a new bug species that would go down in the annals of Crawling Critter's Cyclopedia.

For a moment I felt a twinge of excitement over telling my grandchildren, *"I was there,"* when local newspapers announced, "National Geographic Features Local Shutterbug!"

With seconds ticking away before the light turned green, I focused my attention toward the photographer's prized object. A manhole cover? *No way ... it can't be.* At the last minute, I pulled over to the curb to make sure I saw what I saw. *Yep—a manhole cover, if I ever saw one.*

Wasn't God thoughtful to stop traffic long enough for this writer to witness such a history-making scene?

Prayer Pathway: *God, how amazing that You delight in using the work of our hands, no matter how strange.*

Free to be ...

Scripture Trail: Daniel 1:17, Romans 12:4-5, Ephesians 4:11

Stepping Stone: Romans 12:4

> *"For as we have many members in one body, but all the members do not have the same function,"*

"Different strokes for different folks." What catches one person's eye, causing *oohs and ahs,* may elicit a *yeah whatever* response from another.

I recently made a trip to a large bookstore to spend a gift card. Aisles and aisles of choices spread out before me. Would I buy a bite-your-nails novel? Or how about an in-depth topical Bible study? Books on boats, crafts, science, humor, and pets lined the shelves. The choices revealed the endless range of customers' interests.

Artists occupy a category of *different strokes* all their own. The Arts section in today's newspaper showed a person looking down at what appeared to be a large tire, about five feet in diameter, lying flat on the museum floor. Some kind of stringy fabric covered the rubber. The black and white picture deprived me of delving into the subliminal messages of this artistic statement.

Musicians run the gamut of expression from the blues, to rap, to spirituals, to rock. Guitars, pianos, drums, and flutes reflect just a fraction of the instruments at their disposal. Singers perform in barbershop quartets, opera, as soloists and in choirs. Poets write limericks, haiku, free verse, and rhyme.

I may select from a vast array of *strokes* as I pursue a variety of interests that mirror who I am. The possibilities remain limitless. Back to my gift card ... guess what I bought. A big fat juicy thesaurus, of course! Now, I ask, "Isn't that the most exciting thing in the whole wide world?"

Prayer Pathway: *May I honor You, Father, with every interest and skill You give me.*

Wearing O' the Green

Scripture Trail: Psalm 1:3, Psalm 23:1-3, Song of Solomon 2:13

Stepping Stone: Psalm 23:2

> *"He makes me lie down in green pastures; He leads me beside still waters.'"*

Akiane, a beautiful angel sent to earth, produces stunning works of art. At the age of 8, she painted a picture of Jesus entitled, *Prince of Peace: The Resurrection.* No matter where I stand when viewing this masterpiece, His eyes appear to follow me.

It just so happens, this Jesus painting is also my sister Laurie's favorite. And *it just so happens* that Laurie went to an Akiane exhibit. And *it just so happens* that the Lord prompted a woman, whom Laurie met for the first time, to purchase a $500 print of this picture for her. And now, I am living green with envy.

I know … I know, I'm not supposed to covet. While I am thrilled for Laurie, I'm still a tad bit envious.

My home state of Oregon is known for *living green*. A man once pedaled his bike up next to my car, while I waited at a red light, and signaled me to lower my window. *Did I have a low tire or maybe a tail light out?*

This zealous 'Save the Planet' activist informed me that the metal frame around my license plate weighed a whole pound and that it was of the utmost importance that I remove the frame and recycle it. He wasn't kidding around.

Psalm 23 says the LORD will make me lie down in green pastures. Green with envy, living green, or green pastures … I think the grass always grows greener where The Good Shepherd leads.

Prayer Pathway: *Green with envy … living green … green pastures, may I color my life with shades of green that please You.*

Spontaneous Combustion

Scripture Trail: Numbers 22:27-31, Psalm 16:11, Proverbs 15:15

Stepping Stone: Proverbs 15:15

> *"... but he who has a merry heart has a continual feast."*

Spontaneous people make life entertaining. They test the limits of decorum while managing to *sort of* stay within the boundaries of acceptable behavior. No need to ask Webster for a definition—just look at my friend, Kris.

Laughter follows Kris wherever she goes. *Stuffed shirts* don't stay starched very long around her. They either loosen up or give up.

Kris makes eating at restaurants an experience fit for a comic strip. After finishing a nice lunch together, the two of us didn't want our dining pleasure to end. As a member of the older generation, i.e. anyone over 40, I expected the sensible thing. *We're finished eating, so let's pay the tab and look forward to the next time.*

Tah dah! Miss Spontaneity to the rescue! A goofy food sculpture prolonged our fun. Several minutes later we had created an original work of art from our plates, cups, napkins, forks, spoons, knives and even leftover food. I'm sure the few amused spectators from nearby tables marveled at our finishing touch—a pickle on top.

Kris and I behaved ourselves enough that we made sure our impromptu sculpture wouldn't likely fall over and leave a yucky mess. Somebody had to bus the dishes anyway, right? We just wanted to help stack them—that's all.

While God doesn't have food sculptures in the Bible, He does exhibit the unexpected: Balaam's talking donkey, Aaron's rod budding, Peter walking on water ... and of course, the burning bush—God's version of spontaneous combustion!

Prayer Pathway: *Laughter—what a cool gift from You, God!*

Taking My Medicine

Scripture Trail: Proverbs 12:25, Proverbs 17:22, Philippians 4:6-7

Stepping Stone: Philippians 4:6

> *"Be anxious for nothing, but in everything by prayer and supplication, with thanksgiving, let your request be made known to God;"*

Where's a camera when I need one? Well … there's usually one in a relative's shutterbug's hands. When family parties take place for my clan of 30 to 40 bonafide clowns, *kuh-razy* photo ops abound.

At one of our shindigs, Uncle Arlen knelt down, while Lani, Jacqui, and Becky—three beautiful daughters-of-the-heart—lined up behind him, striking an *Arlen's Angels* pose. These special angels, each over 50, hardly look a day older than when they and Arlen first spoofed the TV trio from *Charlie's Angels* 30 plus years ago.

And how about a hair fight for a parlor trick? Suffice it to say, this prank ranks right up there with snipe hunts. What a great way to initiate a daughter's unsuspecting date to her family. Matt was never the same, but Tyana still got her prince, despite her loony kinfolk.

My friend, Dr. Linda Dunakin, who now hangs out full-time with The Great Physician, frequently offered me a prescription to take on days when I found laughter hard to come by. When physical challenges caused a hitch in my emotional *git-along*, she prescribed Philippians 4:6-7. Next time I came in to see her, she'd smile and ask, "Did you take your medicine?"

Laughter, plus God's Word … hmm … I hear tell in Proverbs 17:22 that, *"A merry heart does good like a medicine."* Next time I need a dose of encouragement, maybe I'll snub Internet cures and do a Scripture search instead. Sounds like good doctoring to me!

Prayer Pathway: *Doctor Jesus, You give the best medicine ever.*

God, I pray that You would use the unique 'me' to:

_____

_____

_____

_____

_____

_____

_____

_____

_____

_____

_____

_____

_____

_____

_____

_____

I lay every burden and joy at the feet of Jesus.

"Next time
I need a dose
of encouragement,
maybe I'll snub
Internet cures
and do a Scripture
search instead."

Laughter

Laughter is truly a curious thing

From nowhere clear it seems to spring

Bubbling over stones in a stream

Dancing down a sun's golden beam

Leaving me breathless, gasping for air

Sweet moments of life without a care

Just when I think I've got control

Another round will within me roll

Try as I might no end can I bring

Laughter is truly a curious thing

Dedicated to my Abba Father
Creator of a donkey that talked
Somersaulting kittens
And penguins in tuxedos

The Old Paths

Steps

Remember the Old Paths

God's Men

The Good Old Days

Giant Leaps

"Soup's on!"

A Cowboy and His Bride

Beyond the Shadows

Home Sweet Home

Time Traveler

"Brrr …"

Fruity People

Dancers on the Water
Poem

"Stand in the ways and see, and ask for the old paths,
where the good way is and walk in it;
then you will find rest for your souls …"
Jeremiah 6:16

Remember the Old Paths

Scripture Trail: Psalm 77:11, Psalm 143:4-8, Jeremiah 6:16

Stepping Stone: Jeremiah 6:16

> *"Thus says the LORD: 'Stand in the ways and see,
> and ask for the old paths where the good way is ..."*

Senior saints. Long before I was one, I looked forward to hearing the stories they passed on to the next generation. Timeless truths lie beyond yarns such as, "Honey, I remember when I walked five miles to school through the snow, uphill both ways."

Retha, a tiny lady of 98, recalled going out with her beau in a surrey with a fringe on top. She also remembered man landing on the moon. Adapting to change, her humor intact, she offered diamonds of resilience through her intriguing stories.

Bob, a dapper gentleman, deferred to the ladies as he invited them to enter doorways first. His chivalry delighted all who knew him. At one time a concert pianist, he exuded sophisticated charm. Although dementia ravaged Bob's mind, gems of kindness still defined him.

Grover declared the goodness of the Lord as he said goodbye to his beloved wife, Betty. He exuded trust even in heartache. His sweet spirit, even through grief, reflected the priceless nugget of peace in life's most painful times.

Mentoring children, exercising their right to vote, delivering food to shut-ins, praying for their children and grandchildren, knowing how to make do with little, reverence before Almighty God ... precious stones of wisdom await young miners. The elder generation has already shed blood, sweat, and tears to discover hidden treasures. Instead of donning a hard hat and grabbing a pickaxe, they invite the younger crowd to simply pull up a chair, set a spell, and hear some of wisdom's riches.

Prayer Pathway: *Lord, I long to listen and learn from my elders the truths that You have shown them.*

God's Men

Scripture Trail: 1 Samuel 16:7, 1 Corinthians 9:19-22, James 4:11

Stepping Stone: 1 Corinthians 9:22

> *"… I have become all things to all men, that I might by all means save some."*

Jeff Dorothy, my former pastor, led the way in sharing Christ with motorcycle riders and gun-totin' cowboys. For several years, on Father's day, a dozen shiny motorcycles parked across the front of the gymnasium where my church holds Sunday morning services. On this particular day, more important than the *oohs* and *ahs* expressed over some very impressive bikes, were the riders who came with them—some who didn't know Jesus.

Just so non-Harley owners don't feel worried, we also welcomed Kawasaki, Triumph, and Honda riders. In fact, anyone who drove a motor of any kind, even a riding lawn mower, qualified for fun as a member of *The Motor Ministry*. There was a place in God's house for all.

On other occasions, a whole passel of cowboys from the Tri-County Gun Club would show up for church. Guys and gals with holsters, wearing chaps and cowboy boots, would come in to take a load off their feet. They'd taken a Sunday away from Cowboy Action Shooting, removing their ten gallon hats in God's house to worship Him. Pastor Jeff—a man's man, shared Christ in a genuine way that said, *I really care about you.*

Pastor Jeff moseyed on down the trail after 22 years of dedicated service. Our new minister, Pastor Larry, brings with him a legacy of mentoring gang bangers and football players—God's man for this hour.

Whether a motorcycle rider, or a football jock … God knows how to get past the helmet to the heart.

Prayer Pathway: *Open my eyes to use whatever means You place in my hands to share Your love.*

The Good Old Days

Scripture Trail: Genesis 24:1, Deuteronomy 32:7, Psalm 90:16-17

Stepping Stone: Deuteronomy 32:7

> *"Remember the days of old, consider the years of many generations. Ask your father, and he will show you; your elders, and they will tell you:"*

Some people say *the good old days* weren't all that good. As a result of life's daily hardships, people didn't advertise every problem that came their way.

Society's concept of what constitutes a crisis has greatly changed in the last 50 years. When our dishwasher broke down, with panic in their baby blues eyes, my children asked, "What are we gonna do?" Washing dishes by hand didn't enter their thinking.

When a dryer belt broke, out the door went bags of wet clothes to dry at the Laundromat. Whatever happened to clothes lines and drying racks? *How archaic.*

In the younger crowds' opinion, a prolonged power outage equals about two hours. Give them 24 hours and great learning opportunities emerge for our darling offspring to experience *life back when.* The world still turns without television and computers. But today's kids don't play fair. Radios and CD players ... oh, excuse me ... make that smartphones and handheld electronic games come to their rescue. All they gotta do is find some batteries, and "Voila!" life is good again.

Nevertheless, when the lights go out, we old fogies shine; we pull out the stops and strut our stuff! Dinners by candlelight, reading by kerosene lamps instead of radios, meals cooked over coals, conserving water in rain barrels, snuggling under piles of blankets—all hark back to simpler times.

Kids, try this on: How about mucking a barn, chopping a cord of wood, and plucking a few chickens before school?" Sounds like fun!

Prayer Pathway: *The elder generation teaching the younger—what a great plan.*

Giant Leaps

Scripture Trail: Psalm 61:1-4, Mark 4:39, Hebrews 13:8

Stepping Stone: Hebrews 13:8

> *"Jesus Christ is the same yesterday, today, and forever."*

"That's one small step for man, one giant leap for mankind." On July 20, 1969, Neil Armstrong and Buzz Aldridge made the first lunar landing. Man *on* the moon replaced the man *in* the moon. Who would've ever thunk it?

In my grandparents' day, sitting in a Model T while zooming down the road at a top speed of 45 miles per hour constituted a big leap. With the advent of rumble seats, courting on horseback went the way of "Happy Trails to You."

Ma Bell went from hand-cranked phones to hands-free cell phones, and now everybody who's anybody has one on their car's dashboard. Digitized voice has upstaged party lines. Carrying a bazillion times more information, underground thread-thin fiber optics uproot telephone poles.

Blue jeans used to come in two choices: 'blue' and 'denim'. End of decision. Now teenagers must choose from every color under the rainbow, wide cut, knee-length, hip huggers, rhinestone studded legs, fringed hems, patched, and whatever else. The holes in jeans that Grandpa earned by working dawn to dusk, youngsters now pay big bucks for, without breaking a sweat.

The world careens from one change to the next. The latest and greatest computer technology becomes outdated in months, instead of years. This 'Age of Change' leaves me feeling disoriented and never quite *with it*.

While the world leaps on the bandwagon for the next new thing that everyone *must have*, I'm so glad that Jesus remains my rock in this turbulent sea of change.

Prayer Pathway: *Jesus, help me remember that You always stay by my side, no matter how 'not with it' I feel.*

"Soup's on!"

Scripture Trail: Psalm 92:14, Psalm 143:5, Zechariah 8:4-5

Stepping Stone: Psalm 92:14

> *"They shall still bear fruit in old age; they shall be fresh and flourishing,"*

Certain "benefits" come with getting older. Age 50 magically marked the starting point for uninvited signals that came my way shouting, "You're getting old!" I started receiving cutesy cards that said, "When I am old, I shall wear purple." I happen to like the color purple, *so there*. But when the AARP magazine showed up in the mailbox, now ... that wasn't funny.

How well I remember teasing Arlen, when he hit the *big 5-0*. Just like clockwork, his free AARP magazine arrived. Five years later, when some micromanaging person sent me my very own copy for my 50th ... well, I decided they had way too much time on their hands. They wouldn't have heard one complaint from me had they left me out.

Beyond free magazines, aging comes with additional benefits. When I plead 'senior moment' at forgetting things, people smile at my excuses. Even though my *forgetter* kicks in more often with each passing year, I still enjoy an increasing supply of memories that haven't leaked out the floorboards of my cranial storehouse.

I don't go back to the days of hand-pumped water, wood burning ovens, and cylinder records. But, I can still hear the words of an old song, "Precious memories, how they linger ...." Poodle skirts, personal letters that outnumbered junk mail, parking on the ice cream churner until my bottom felt frozen, and ... and ... and ...

I think I smell a simmering pot of memory soup. Smells mighty good!

Prayer Pathway: *How loving of You, Lord, to wrap up sweet memories in the package of old age.*

A Cowboy and His Bride

Scripture Trail: Deuteronomy 6:6-9, Proverbs 3:5, 1 Peter 5:5

Stepping Stone: Deuteronomy 6:7

> *"You shall teach them [these words] diligently to your children, and shall talk of them when you sit in your house …"*

My earliest memories include listening to my childhood pastor, Lee Brock and his bride, Frances, read daily devotions. I always felt so special when I went to their house for lunch after church. At their home, for the first time as a child, I experienced regular Bible readings and prayer.

More than 50 years later, when I visit them, I close my eyes and listen to their soft Texas drawl as they read Scripture and pray for missionaries. Once again, I'm a child sitting at their feet.

Whether behind a pulpit or preaching at an assisted living, this cowpoke preacher still stands tall, wearing a suit with a bolo tie—and his cowboy boots. He humbly urges his flock to stay on the trail that leads to eternal life.

Brother Brock relives the habits of many a trail hand who wrote poetry by a campfire, after a long day of herding cattle. This cowboy bard asks important questions such as: *"Did Mordecai Ride an Appaloosa?"* In his poem entitled, *Texas*, Lee spins an ode to The Lone Star state, of longhorn cattle, of rattlesnakes, and cactus. In another, this cowpoke thanks the Lord for *The Old Windmill* where he and his horse quenched their thirst.

After a long day in my city slicker saddle, I often think of an old cowboy and his Texas darlin'. Lee and Frances faithfully follow the trail that leads to Jesus' final roundup—and as a part of their legacy—so will I.

Prayer Pathway: *God, where would I be without those who led me to You when I was just a young cowgirl?*

Beyond the Shadows

Scripture Trail: Isaiah 64:4, 1 Corinthians 13:12, 1 John 3:1-2

Stepping Stone: 1 Corinthians 13:12

> *"For now we see in a mirror, dimly, but then face to face. Now I know in part, but then I shall know just as I also am known."*

It's early morning. Across my living room, I see shadows moving against the narrow white slats of the closed blinds. Silhouettes of tree branches covered with leaves dance in the morning breeze. The outline of full bushes nestles against the house. Sunbeams shine, welcoming a new day; yet I only see a hint of their glimmering brightness.

When I later open the shades, I will see what lies beyond the shadows. The tree will display emerald green leaves dancing against the brown bark of its branches and trunk. The sun's brightness will no longer hide behind a veiled window. Its brilliant rays will burst through the glass, no longer obscured by manmade limitations.

Beyond the shadows, I know that greater beauty awaits me. I've seen what lies on the other side of my living room blinds. Lovely rhododendron bushes, lush in white and pink blossoms, grow just outside. Perhaps I'll see the squirrel I hear chattering at a pesky blue jay. At this moment, I can only imagine the two of them chasing each other through the network of tree limbs.

Someday—some wonderful day—I will at last see beyond the shadows of this life on earth. Jesus will lift the curtain. I will see heaven unfold before my eyes, in all its beauty and regal splendor. I'll hear Jesus tender voice speaking to me, "Welcome home, my dear one."

I will see Him face to face. No more shadows. Only my dear Lord.

Prayer Pathway: *Lord, how I long to see beyond the shadows of this earth and behold Your glorious beauty.*

Home Sweet Home

Scripture Trail: John 14:23, 2 Corinthians 5:1-2, Hebrews 11:16

Stepping Stone: Hebrews 11:16

> *"But now they desire a better, that is, a heavenly country. Therefore God is not ashamed to be called their God, for He has prepared a city for them."*

The farmhouse I grew up in sat atop a hill, surrounded by 450 acres of farmland. A one-room schoolhouse sat nestled at the bottom of the hill. No longer used for educating the area youngsters, my sister, Minnie Belle, made it a homey place for raising her children.

Irrigation pipes covered the fields. Combines and haying trucks dotted the landscape. Cows stood in the fields chewing their cud, thinking deep bovine thoughts. Horses pranced across the pastures, their tails blowing in the wind.

My big brother, Larry, and I commiserate over the demise of the old homestead. The farmhouse and barns are gone. Paved roads replace gravel driveways. State-of-the-art schools long ago gobbled up the one-room schoolhouse. Cars far outnumber any cows and horses that ever roamed the fields. Pastures have morphed into upscale suburban neighborhoods

Sadness engulfs me when I go back to visit the countryside that now exists only in my memories. I feel as though something holy has been desecrated. While all around me the familiar disappears, I increasingly understand that this world is not my home. Like it or not, I can't recreate those magic places of my childhood.

Jesus knew how much His children would need a forever place to call home. And so He came to visit mankind and then returned to His heavenly dwelling to prepare a wonderful place, with me the focus of His loving hands. And when I get there, I will *know in my knower*—I am home at last.

Prayer Pathway: *Master Builder, I'm so glad that You've prepared a home—sweet home—just for me.*

Time Traveler

Scripture Trail: Exodus 33:11, Isaiah 41:8, John 15:13-15,

Stepping Stone: John 15:15

> *"... I have called you friends, for all things that I heard from My father I have made known to you."*

While protestors marked the sixties, two airmen quietly served their country. They came from hometowns just three hours apart in Oregon and Washington. God had plans that they meet 2,500 miles away in Biloxi, Mississippi at Keesler Air Force Base. And so began a friendship that has spanned 50 years.

David married Melba, his high school sweetheart, soon followed by Arlen, my handsome man in Air Force blues, marrying me. Within a couple decades, David and Melba added Monte, Jon, Melodie, Joy, and Heidi to 'Harmony Haven' while the Peacocks' nest filled up with our seven peachicks.

I look back on a half century of friendship—the mountaintops and the valleys. Our son, Larry, made his grand entrance on Monte's 10th birthday. Two days later, we entered a dark valley when baby Joy was born. She lived for just over two months, every day of her brief life a gift to all who loved her.

I smile over memories of playing cards with David, affectionately dubbed 'Turtle'. He now bravely faces each day with the challenges of Parkinson's disease. My *bud*, Melba, and I held each other's hand through our cancer battles. We've laughed and cried on long road trips, and often rescued each other from the next cake decorating deadline.

Laughter and tears fill the years we've shared. I gasp to think that Jesus, the Lord of all creation, travels beyond time, making the impossible possible. With all that friendship means, He chooses to call me *'Friend'*.

Prayer Pathway: *Lord, my heart stops when I consider the gift of friendship that You extend to me.*

"Brrr ..."

Scripture Trail: Philippians 4:11, 1 Timothy 6:8, Hebrews 13:5

Stepping Stone: 1 Timothy 6:8

> *"And having food and clothing, with these we shall be content;"*

Stuart Hamblen must have known the Pursel family when he wrote the song, *This Old House*. A couple lines go:
This old house lets in the rain
This old house lets in the cold
Pastor Larry and Terrie, and their sons, Trevor and Connor, set down roots in a dilapidated parsonage when they accepted the call to pastor a small church. Their new abode soon challenged their family motto: *God has provided this for us. It is enough.*

Lacking a furnace, three space heaters helped them not become the frozen chosen. When freezing winds blew, their curtains moved. After stormy weather, Trevor and Connor had fun seeing how many roof tiles they would find outside the next day.

Twice, Pastor Larry and Terrie discovered black soot streaking up from an outlet—once when they got up in the morning, and once when they arrived home from an outing.

Hats on their heads, snuggled in layers of sweaters, and wrapped up in blankets, the Pursel family played board games on the floor. Their competitive spirits kept their minds off the cold.

After seven-and-a-half years living in this memorable home, Mom, Dad, and boys finally moved to a comfortable house. But, Trevor and Connor got an A+ in the lessons they learned from their parents when one winter day they asked, "Can we open all the windows, turn off the heat, wrap up in blankets, and play games on the floor like we used to?"

Ahh ... for the good old days.

Prayer Pathway: *Lord, I want to remember Your goodness, even in the midst of hard times.*

Fruity People

Scripture Trail: Deuteronomy 30:9-10, Hosea 14:8, John 15:8

Stepping Stone: John 15:8

> *"'By this My Father is glorified, that you bear much fruit; so you will be My disciples.'"*

Fruity people. From the produce of their personal storehouses, they scout for opportunities to bless others.

Forrest Franklin, Arlen's childhood pastor, and his wife, Bertha, were fruity people. When we visited them, we never left without a gift in hand, usually a Christian book from their prized collection. In the course of their long lives, they planted a love for God's word that bore fruit in thousands of hearts.

Dennis and Charlotte Bischof epitomize humility. For 25 years they've gone to migrant camps, delivering food and clothing—along with the gospel. Heaven will need a huge party room just to accommodate the guest list of sixteen hundred plus people who have found Christ through their selfless service.

Some truly sweet fruitcakes … *oops, I mean fruity people,* include Norman and Betty Dancer. While Norm, ever the master punster, would readily own up to the 'fruitcake' label, Betty deserves a purple heart for her ever-enduring spirit. I cannot guess how many lives their generosity has touched.

Moving from Washington to Oregon, to Colorado, to Connecticut, to Minnesota, and back to Oregon, I have been touched by the love of my brothers and sisters in Christ. Even brief visits with family and fellow believers in Florida and Texas forever enriched my faith.

I'm so glad I will have endless hours in heaven to personally thank every precious one for their impact on my life. Fruity people … what a bountiful harvest they'll one day lay at the feet of Jesus.

Prayer Pathway: *Father, I ask You to produce abundant fruit in my life that will touch the lives of others for eternity.*

I look back and recall the people and circumstances that led me to You:

_____

_____

_____

_____

_____

_____

_____

_____

_____

_____

_____

_____

_____

_____

_____

I lay every burden and joy at the feet of Jesus.

"Whether a motorcycle rider, or a football jock ... God knows how to get past the helmet to the heart."

Dancers on the Water

The lighthouse shines its beam
O'er stormy seas or still
Guiding wand'ring ships to shore
Its beacon—a mission to fulfill
  And night after night
    Its rays of hope
      Dancing
        Dancing
          Dancing on the water

The lighthouse of friendship true
Formed by our Father's hands
Gives to hearts healing streams of love
Through life's winds and shifting sands
  And year after year
    Their rays of hope
      Dancing
        Dancing
          Dancing on the water

The Lighthouse of our soul
Stands strong through ev'ry time and season
Drawn to His saving light of love
Its depths beyond all reason
  And forever and ever
    His rays of hope
      Dancing
        Dancing
          Dancing on the water

Dedicated to Norman & Elizabeth Dancer
with gratitude for your love and generosity

Following Him

Steps

"Wrong number, please."

Box Upon Box

Randy

"You first ... I insist!"

Percolating Perks

Blue Angels

"Somebody, fence me in!"

Stammering Lips and Fingertips

"Nn ... now?"

"Pardon me ... pretty please?"

Creature Comforts

You've Made a Difference
Poem

"... Obey My voice, and I will be your God,
and you shall be My people ..."
Jeremiah 7:23

"Wrong number, please."

Scripture Trail: John 13:35, John 15:12, 1 Corinthians 13:3-8

Stepping Stone: John 13:35

> *"By this all will know that you are my disciples, if you have love for one another."*

Ring ... ring. I brushed flour off my hands and answered the phone. Let a call go? *Perish the thought!*

"Hello."

"Did you used to have the number, 503-644-XXXX? We have your old number now and we're getting a lot of calls for you."

Gulp. "Well, yes ... that was our number." My stomach churned. Hand me the Tums. I could hear it now: *I'd like a nickel for every call I've taken for you. Why don't people know your number by now? How come I'm the lucky one to get the number of someone who knows half of Oregon? I oughta yank my phone off the wall!* Double gulp.

After living in one area for 40 years, my runaway fears couldn't be far off the mark. Ma Bell had been too quick in assigning our previous number to this unfortunate woman. Her voice came back on the line: "May I give your number to people who call? You guys must be Christians. All your callers are so polite."

Say what? I would have turned up my hearing aid, if I used one. I mumbled my permission and hung up the receiver. Had I heard her right? Maybe she was pulling my leg. Or how about *Candid Camera*? No, that was ancient history.

Jesus said that the world would know we are Christians by our love for one another. How grateful I am for friends and family who represent Christ so well.

By the way, my new number is ...

Prayer Pathway: *Lord, may my life reflect Your love, even in small things like answering the phone.*

Box upon Box

Scripture Trail: Isaiah 28:9-10, Luke 19:17, Philippians 4:9

Stepping Stone: Isaiah 28:10

> *"For precept must be upon precept, precept upon precept, line upon line, line upon line, here a little, there a little."*

"It's a messy job, but somebody's gotta do it." I jumped in to help my foster sisters move out of their mother's two thousand square foot house. My second Mom lived there 34 years, raised five daughters, and kept an open door for people who needed help. As an elementary school teacher, Doris saved endless boxes of wonderful *doodads*, and *whatchamacallits* for her students.

Doris' house had lots of rooms, closets, an attic, and a garage—all packed full with stuff. *Stuff* proliferated like dandelions. We would just get some *stuff* out of the house and more *stuff* sneaked up right behind us. *Stuff … stuff … and more stuff.*

Precept upon precept—room upon room, we sorted. *Line upon line*—closet upon closet, we boxed more *stuff. Here a little, there a little*—we packed and put away *stuff.* Finally, the moment came when the last container went out the door.

Only once did Arlen and I jump into building a house. While contracting out some of the work, we put a lot of sweat equity into its completion. One room at a time, including lots of tears and sore muscles, we moved in a year later.

In my life's journey, I've experienced problems that seemed unsolvable—goals that appeared unattainable. Raising a large family proved a closet at a time, a day at a time, deal. Each sunrise presented new challenges that I had to meet.

Line upon line, prayer upon prayer, I grow closer to Jesus.

Prayer Pathway: *Savior, with each day that passes, I want to do my part to know You better.*

Randy

Scripture Trail: 2 Chronicles 15:7, Joel 3:10, 2 Corinthians 12:9-10

Stepping Stone: 2 Corinthians 12:9

> *"And He said to me, 'My grace is sufficient for you, for My strength is made perfect in weakness.'"*

Randy celebrated his last birthday with a party in heaven. Here on earth, he hobnobbed with The Beach Boys, Dallas Cowboy cheerleaders, and Will Vinton of the California Raisins. Randy even received letters from every President since Ronald Reagan. All of this pales in comparison to Randy's triumphal run into the arms of Jesus on his 42nd birthday.

Randy's parents, Bill and Diane, rejoice in the 31 bonus years they had with their precious son. When diagnosed with leukemia, doctors gave Randy an estimated six months to live. He underwent a transplant using his sister, Lori's, bone marrow. Randy faithfully expressed his gratitude to Lori every anniversary of the transplant.

Multiple physical challenges could not deter Randy from a life filled with love and purpose. Detached retinas in both eyes impaired his vision. Spinal meningitis devastated his hearing. Complications from his bone marrow transplant caused his skin to contract so he was unable to straighten his legs and fingers. In spite of Randy's physical limitations, he became a gifted artist and computer whiz. He enjoyed life and did not consider himself handicapped.

Known as Pastor Web, Randy maintained his church website while also giving encouragement over the Internet to countless people suffering chronic and life-threatening illnesses.

Randy loved the Lord, had a strong Christian faith, and a great sense of humor. A dab of whipped cream on the tip of his nose left more than one friend squirming at restaurants.

Wonderful in weakness, Randy made life one grand adventure.

Prayer Pathway: *Thank You for those in my life that teach me how to lean on Your strength in weakness.*

"You first … I insist!"

Scripture Trail: Romans 12:10, Philippians 2:1-4, 1 Timothy 4:12

Stepping Stone: Philippians 2:4

> *"Let each of you look out not only for his own interests, but also for the interests of others."*

My son, Larry, is a basketball fanatic. During my pregnancy with him, he dribbled a basketball full court. For many years, the orange orb seemed an extension of his hand. Through four years of college ball, I rarely saw Larry without a basketball glued to his palm. He played until his legs wanted to quit and still went back for more. Making a showy slam-dunk was his notion of soaring straight to heaven.

During high school, life got even more exciting for Larry when he played a charity game against several alumni of the Portland Trailblazers. Even these pros couldn't intimidate my young 'baller'. One of the Blazers, seeing Larry's intensity for the game, gave him a nod as if to say, "Go for it, Kid."

Allowing Larry to go for a dunk, this Trailblazer knew—and Larry knew—that the opportunity to strut his stuff was a gift. Even so, my bouncing ball handler came up beaming after making an impressive dunk against a Blazer player. I will long remember Larry's ecstatic smile.

Nineteen years have come and gone since the benefit basketball game that filled an evening with light-hearted fun. Just as easily it could have been an ego trip for the professionals and a *why-bother* experience for the amateur opponents. As a spectator, I felt blessed by the graciousness of our local sports celebrities. As a mother, I shared in the joy of my son's moment of glory—all because of the kindness of a pro.

Prayer Pathway: *May I delight in helping others to excel.*

Percolating Perks

Scripture Trail: Matthew 7:7-11, John 10:10, Ephesians 3:20

Stepping Stone: John 10:10

> *"The thief does not come except to steal, and to kill, and to destroy. I have come that they may have life, and that they may have it more abundantly."*

Perks. Employers dangle these carrots to entice qualified workers. Employees relish these side benefits that extend beyond their paychecks. Perks come in lots of packages.

> ➢ Airline employees fly for free.
> ➢ College employees receive reduced or free tuition.
> ➢ Fitness centers give free membership.

Just as employers offer benefits beyond the standard take-home pay, God blesses me with perks that exceed my greatest expectations. My heavenly Father and full-time employer specializes in creative management with benefits only He can give.

> ➢ In adversity, He gives me joy unspeakable.
> ➢ He gives enduring hope, no matter my circumstance.
> ➢ He loves me, even when I fail Him.
> ➢ Bonuses apply beginning on the start date.

When I signed-up for God's payroll, He blessed me beyond all I could think or ask. When I show up at His doorstep, I need not fear age, gender, or race discrimination. I'll always see a sign posted: "Applications being accepted." When I mess up (not if), He doesn't fire me, but instead, with words of encouragement He sets me back on my feet. His job reviews come based on grace, not performance. His retirement plan lasts for eternity with no age requirements to receive full benefits. He never puts me out to pasture.

With abundant perks always in the planning by The One who never gives me a pink slip, how can I lose by signing on with Him? Applications are available upon request by going to: HisWord.communicationwith.Him. Immediate response guaranteed.

Prayer Pathway: *God, Your perks beat anything this world has to offer.*

Blue Angels

Scripture Trail: Proverbs 10:17, Romans 13:1-3, 1 Peter 2:13

Stepping Stone: Romans 13:1

> *"Let every soul be subject to the governing authorities. For there is no authority except from God, and the authorities that exist are appointed by God."*

"You're not going to tell me you didn't see that stop sign." I wilted as the polite, but stern, officer in blue bent down and looked straight at me. Somehow I knew that this guy wouldn't fall for any female tears, though I could have produced some without trying.

Wanting to hide under the car's floorboard, I restrained my thoughts that fought to escape my lips. *Oh no, officer—not in a million years would I tell you I didn't see that flat red lollipop sticking up at the street corner.*

Truth is … I didn't see it. The scene he rightfully saw? Not one obstruction obscured the stop sign. No trees. No shrubs. Wouldn't you know it, not one single elephant blocked this traffic marker.

Please, no laughing at my alibi. As my car approached the sign, the sun blinded my eyes. Painfully true. Was I still guilty? Absolutely.

Adding to my ruffled feathers, I'd just done a good deed for a sick friend. And the clincher to my frustration? Had my health permitted, I could have walked home from my friend's house.

With a clean driving record, the city clerk greatly reduced my fine. Nevertheless, pay the piper I did. Maybe I should chalk up my blunder to *a bad glare day*. The take-no-guff officer was God's angel protecting others from drivers like me. Thankfully, the infraction hurt nothing more than my pride and my pocketbook.

I reckon S-T-O-P means, "**S**top, **T**hink, **O**r, **P**ay!"

Prayer Pathway: *When I need correction, help me show respect toward the authorities You place in my life.*

"Somebody, fence me in!"

Scripture Trail: 1 Chronicles 4:10, Job 38:8-11, Psalm 89:9

Stepping Stone: Job 38:11

> *"When I said, 'This far you may come, but no farther,*
> *and here your proud waves must stop!'"*

Suppose I lived in a world without boundaries? Children excel at expressing that question. "Why can't I have a candy bar before dinner?" The peanuts in a Snickers bar qualify as protein, right? And the *milk* chocolate must satisfy the dairy group.

"Why can't I stay up as late as I want?" Teenagers behave as though sleep is highly overrated, *until* work needs doing.

"Why can't I drive my friends to the beach? After all, I've had my license a whole two months!"

Grown-up kids see no reason they can't have their car and pay for it with their good looks. "I've worked hard and I really owe myself a new Hummer. Besides, the next time there's an earthquake, I can play the hero and drive everyone to safety, no matter the road conditions.

Never mind that I've robbed Peter to pay Paul for the last three years. Poor Peter. He always gets the bum end of the deal.

If I'm not pushing the limits for scrumptious taste treats, unrestricted hours, or break-the-bank cars, there's always the spiritual performance-on-demand trap waiting to ensnare me. There are so many *good* things to do, but never enough hours in the day. "Sure, I'll be glad to teach that class, to plan that party, to serve on that committee, and produce twenty decorated cakes for the bake sale to support missions." *Ouch*! Twenty cakes, with six youngsters under foot at the time. Color me red. Guilty as charged.

Limits ... what a concept.

Prayer Pathway: *May I set reasonable limits, remembering that You are God and not me.*

Stammering Lips and Fingertips

Scripture Trail: Daniel 7:14, Zephaniah 3:9, John 16:24-28

Stepping Stone: Zephaniah 3:9

> *"For then I will restore to the peoples a pure language, that they all may call on the name of The LORD, to serve Him with one accord."*

Warning: *Learning a second language may prove hazardous to your reputation.* Those who have taken on this challenge know whereof I speak.

Sign Language, though uniquely graceful, nevertheless provides fuel for fumbling. As an employee for a community college, I interpreted an algebra class where the professor explained the term πr^2. This mathematical formula has its own specific signs but, for a few seconds, my brain took a lunch break. What flowed off my fingertips was, "Pie are square." Immediately, I realized my mistake. To my relief, just before my *faux pas* happened, the deaf student looked down at her textbook and didn't see my blunder. Nevertheless, I spent the rest of the class time sucking it in, while I squelched the urgent need to laugh.

A budding preacher and fellow student of Sign Language consoled me with his brilliant blooper. Early in his sermonizing/signing career he waxed eloquent about the devil's schemes. Unfortunately, only a slight difference exists between the signs for *devil* and *horse*: bent fingers for *devil* and straight fingers for *horse*. Yes, he did it. He verbally preached—while signing the whole sermon about the temptations of *the horse*.

What a relief to know God is multi-lingual. When I talk to Him, He deals with whatever slip-ups escape my lips, or my fingertips. But I still beg that no one ask me to sign the line from an old hymn: "Here I raise mine Ebenezer." My friend's *horse* just might look tame in comparison.

Prayer Pathway: *Lord, teach me to commune with You in the language of Your heart.*

"Nn ... now?"

Scripture Trail: 1 Samuel 2:35, Matthew 4:20, Luke 12:42-44

Stepping Stone: Matthew 4:20

> *"They immediately left their nets and followed Him."*

Mom tells Joey, "Clean your room before you go out to play."

His baby blues widen. "Nn...now?"

"Yes. Now, Son." Joey's lower lip quivers as he ponders an escape. Then he stomps off in a heartrending exit.

My adult kid, i.e. my husband, does what I call his Fonzie version of "Now?" *The Fonz* from the television program, *Happy Days*, didn't have a problem saying, "Now." But the word, wrong? Well, that was a different story. "I'm wr ... wronnng ..." got stuck somewhere between Fonzie's tonsils and his lips, every time.

Now has only three letters, but for some odd reason, the first letter renders Arlen tongue-tied, especially when I ask him to take out the trash. His reply? "Nn ... nnn ... now?"

"Yes, *now*, dear."

"N ... now? Don't ask me to take out the garbage when I'm headed out the door to work with my hands full!"

O ... kay. Next time I waited until after Arlen's workday. His hands were pure-D empty. "Would you take out the trash, please?"

"Nnn ... nnn ... now? I just got in the door!"

"Uh ... well. So when's a good time for you?"

Arlen stared at me a minute, his brain connecting the dots. He flashed his best *naughty boy* grin. "Any time, but nn ... nn ... now!"

I wonder if Jesus' disciples felt tempted to ask, "Nnn ... nnn ... now?" when the Savior called them to follow Him.

He beckoned. They went. No questions asked.

Prayer Pathway: *Jesus, when I hear You call, may I quickly obey without question.*

"Pardon me … pretty please?"

Scripture Trail: Luke 6:36-37, Acts 24:16, 2 Corinthians 6:3

Stepping Stone: 2 Corinthians 6:3

> *"We give no offense in anything, that our ministry may not be blamed."*

When are those kids going to learn to close the door? Were they born in a barn? My mother shut the front door and then headed to the kitchen to finish making dinner. Unbeknownst to her, at that same moment, her close friend was strolling up the sidewalk for a neighborly visit.

The door closed in Mary Ann's face, and she walked away, hurt and refusing to speak to my mother for weeks. As time passed, Mom agonized over the obvious rift between them, until she cornered her friend and cleared up the misunderstanding.

Offense. Teenagers act as lightning rods for taking up offenses, both for themselves and on behalf of their friends. A wrong look … boy dumps girl … girl dumps boy, and soon a half-dozen comrades-in-arms commiserate over the injustice of it all. A few weeks later, the next cuter-than-life heartthrob soothes their overwhelming angst. All pain is forgotten—until a new perceived wrong happens.

Movers and shakers vent their anger over the one who steps past them to a higher rung on the corporate ladder. *Doesn't the boss see real talent right under his big nose?* Never mind that the person with the promotion worked sixty-hour weeks to earn his or her new status at the office.

How easy to waste energy on misunderstandings and plain old mistakes. How often have I spoken in haste and immediately wished for a bag over my head?

Judge not … a sure-fire cure for hoof and mouth disease.

Prayer Pathway: *When I put my foot in my mouth, please send someone to help me extricate my size 8s.*

Creature Comforts

Scripture Trail: Isaiah 35:6, Malachi 4:2, 1 Peter 1:6-8

Stepping Stone: Malachi 4:2 (NIV)

> *"you who revere my name, the sun of righteousness will rise with healing in its wing. And you will go out and leap like calves released from the stall."*

"Hello. You've reached the home of the Weiss family and Rick, The Wonder Dog. Well ... sometimes he just makes you wonder."

My friends' telephone greeting always made me chuckle. Perhaps one reason God created cute furry critters was to offer comic relief for His stressed-out, two-legged creatures. Bantering favorite animal stories back and forth with friends melts away tension from my hectic days. The tales to tell of wagging tails seem endless. Outbursts of laughter are a sure thing when sharing crazy pet antics."

How many times have I seen kittens somersault with joy over being alive? Our daughter's cat chirped like a bird just before pouncing on a flashlight beam aimed at the floor. One minute kitty paws fled from sudden noises; the next little Felix stretched out in sweet repose, his legs tucked snug against his stomach.

My dad once received a donkey in payment for helping a lady in a car accident. This attention-craved animal served as a welcoming committee for my school bus. He brayed each time the yellow limousine made its twice daily appearance.

A sweet-scented payback for my practical joker husband poked its pointy little nose from a box wrapped in birthday paper. The for-real skunk, Rosie Greenbaum, made her great escape outdoors a month later.

A kitten curled up purring in my lap. Laughter over an obnoxious donkey. A skunk skittering by with is tail in the air. Surely God chuckled when He blessed His kids with cuteness in creature comforts.

Prayer Pathway: *Father, You did such a delightful thing when You created critters that tickle my funny bone.*

What is the Holy Spirit teaching me in this season of my life's journey?

I lay every burden and joy at the feet of Jesus.

"How easy
to waste energy
on misunderstandings
and plain old
mistakes."

You've Made a Difference

With words so tender and filled with grace
On the wings of your prayers
Hope found a resting place
Touching my heart
Turning my eyes
To behold His face
You've made a difference in my life

With eyes so knowing, acquainted with pain
On the whisper of witness
Joy found a resting place
Touching my sorrow
Calming my fear
To behold His mercy
You've made a difference in my life

With arms so gentle, you held me near
On the winds of your love
Peace found a resting place
Touching my spirit
Lifting my soul
To behold His grace
You've made a difference in my life

Dedicated to Rochelle Weiss

You have taught me so much
about trusting God
through pain and suffering.
Thank you for the difference
you have made in my life.

"Fear ... take a hike!"

Steps

Behind the Mask

Shell-shocked

Playing Chicken

Am I Ready?

"Oil my memory, please!"

God's Got My Number

"Move, mountain … move!"

"But God …"

Transformers

Comfort Zone

Gone Fishin'

At His Mercy
Poem

*"For He shall give His angels charge over you,
to keep you in all your ways."*
Psalm 91:11

Behind the Mask

Scripture Trail: Deuteronomy 31:6-8, Joshua 1:9, Psalm 27:5

Stepping Stone: Deuteronomy 31:8

> *"And the LORD, 'He is the One who goes before you. He will be with you, He will not leave you nor forsake you; do not fear nor be dismayed.'"*

People amaze me. I'm not thinking of daring mountain climbers who dangle over bottomless crevices. The lion tamer who sticks his head into the king of beast's gaping jaws doesn't make this list either. Nor do men and women who yell "Geronimo!" and jump from airplanes rate a place in this Who's Who accounting of incredible individuals. While I shake my head in disbelief at stuntmen's feats and weightlifters' grunts, there's still a category of 'remarkable' that excels even their noteworthy achievements.

A mother gets up each day and smiles for her children while she wonders if her husband's job will survive the latest corporate belt-tightening. Mom still cleans house, supervises homework, and kisses owies as though she has not a care in the world. Never mind that the cupboards are almost empty.

A father punches the time clock fifty weeks a year, rarely taking a sick day, even when he should. Year after year, he socks away savings so that someday his children can go to college and have successful futures. They seldom see Dad's weariness.

A teenager hits the books after a full day of school and working a part-time job. He hides the verbal abuse he faces at home. Neither his teachers, nor friends, know the pain that his quick wit covers. One day he hopes to teach underprivileged kids.

Everyday adults and *everyday* kids walk past me, wearing *everyday* smiles. And hidden, where no one can see, they carry a card that says: 'PhD in Courage'.

Prayer Pathway: *May I look past the masks people wear to see and appreciate courageous hearts all around me.*

Shell-shocked

Scripture Trail: Psalm 37:8, Proverbs 16:32, Ephesians 4:26-27

Stepping Stone: Proverbs 16:32

> *"He who is slow to anger is better than the mighty, and he who rules his spirit than he who takes a city."*

"It was a dark and stormy night." Okay. So it was the middle of the afternoon and the sun was shining. But that's beside the point. $769.34—as in *seven-HUNDRED-sixty-nine dollars and thirty-four cents*—showed up on our cell phone bill.

As in, "Scrape me off the ceiling!" I handed the offending missive to my unsuspecting husband and prayed he had a strong heart and a VERY good explanation.

Arlen's face paled and his eyes bugged out as he stared at the pretty little numbers printed so neatly from some big corporate computer's guts. "No way … this isn't possible. I know I entered the order correctly … *didn't I?*" His voice trailed off to a whisper.

My stomach clenched at the unconvincing tone of his last two words. And *of course* he was running late for work … and *of course* I had no clue how to make his computer cough up the on-line order, and *of course* I just knew our cell phone service would be cut off any second.

There, I got that off my chest.

Breathe in … breathe out … breathe in … breathe out.

One *very very very* (sorry, not good writing, I know) long night and day later, an underpaid call center employee found the problem. Believe it or not, the mistake was theirs—and during my chat with the nice man, I even kept my cool. Give that hero a fat juicy raise and give me a lesson in trusting God.

Prayer Pathway: *When I'm ready to panic and blow my top, send Your sweet Spirit to put a lid on it.*

Playing Chicken

Scripture Trail: Isaiah 41:10-13, Daniel 10:19, Joel 2:21

Stepping Stone: Isaiah 41:13

> *"For I, the LORD your God, will hold your right hand, saying to you, 'Fear not, I will help you.'"*

Cats make great pretend people. Many exude affection, but others try the aloof act. Some felines have high energy, whilst others curl up for frequent catnaps. One of mine plays the mighty mouser, even as the other runs from its shadow.

Sometimes, I'm a bigger fraidy cat than my kitty. One night, just before heading to bed, I placed a package of frozen chicken on the counter to thaw. Originally, the pieces came packaged in a Styrofoam tray. After using half the fresh chicken, I left the remainder in the package, bending the empty half of the tray back over the chicken, sandwich-style. I then covered the meat in plastic wrap before freezing the rest.

Insomnia later paid me a visit, so I got up to read. Before long, a crackling noise snapped in the silence. My *Nervous Nelly* kitten, and even my *Everything's Cool* cat, raised their hackles. Their wide eyes and stalking posture added to my jumpy nerves.

I soon discovered my thawing "chicken sandwich" unfolding, causing the Styrofoam to snap, crackle, and pop. With the house so quiet, the crackling chicken tray echoed in the eerie darkness. My two cats, one on the attack, the other in panic mode, stared at their foe as if to say, "You make one wrong move, Bucko, and you're history."

I laughed at myself as much as I laughed at my *go-get'm* guard cats. How many times do I fear things that harbor no more danger than my cracklin' chicken?

Prayer Pathway: *When I feel afraid, I will lean on Your Word that reminds me, "Fear not."*

Am I Ready?

Scripture Trail: Matthew 24:42, Luke 21:33, 2 Peter 3:10-12

Stepping Stone: 2 Peter 3:10

> *"But the day of the Lord will come as a thief in the night ... both the earth and the works that are in it will be burned up."*

"Houston, we have a problem. Our instruments show a major malfunction. Do you copy?"

"Yes, we copy. What is your status?"

"Houston, our outdoor reading here in Oregon shows 671 degrees, as in Fahrenheit. Do you copy?"

"Yes. Restate your reading, Oregon."

"That's six hundred seventy-one degrees Fahrenheit, Houston, as in 6-7-1. Waiting for further instructions."

Out for a drive one hot summer day, I pulled up to a stoplight and noticed a reader board that flashed the date: August 10. *Ok, works for me.* Next, I watched the time scroll by. I glanced at my watch. *Yep, that's a match.* Then I waited for the temperature reading and thought, "Wow, it's been hot lately. I bet those crawling numbers will read over 100°." With our summer heat wave, the mercury hit three digits for weeks and even 105° the day before.

I blinked and looked at the bright red LED numbers again. 671°? Hold the phone! Had the world ended and we robust souls cruising around in air-conditioned comfort lived to tell about it? This sizzling mind bender left me with fried brain cells, not to mention a serious question. Did Jesus come back and I got left behind big time?

Three weeks later, the reader board still needs some technician's tweaking. I drive by and see the temp still hovering way past meltdown and my head says, "Yikes! This day's one hot puppy!" But my heart says, "Thanks, God for the wakeup call."

Prayer Pathway: *Whenever You return, Jesus, how glad I am that I need not fear that You will leave without me.*

"Oil my memory, please!"

Scripture Trail: Isaiah 26:8, John 14:25-27, Philippians 1:3

Stepping Stone: John 14:26

> *"But the Helper, the Holy Spirit ... He will teach you all things, and bring to your remembrance all things that I said to you."*

I've just raised the bar on what a wife may expect her husband to remember. This tactic will assuredly cause his face to register a worried look that says, *Oh no, what important date did I forget this time?* Try this on for sure-fire results.

After finishing an oil change, the overworked car mechanic forgot to put a new sticker in the window for my next service date. I mentioned this to him, so he replaced the old sticker with a new one, indicating a date three months down the road. Noticing 4-20-13 written neatly with a permanent marker, I did a double take—my wedding anniversary.

Move the big hand forward five hours. My care-free husband helped his tired wife change the bed sheets. With no mischief intended ... well, maybe just an *itsy bitsy* bit, I asked him, "Do you know what three months from today is?" *Where's my camera?*

Arlen took a long pause before he answered, "Uh ... no. What IS three months from today?"

"Our anniversary, of course!" He went from amused disbelief to consternation, as if to say, "You aren't serious ... are you?" I couldn't suppress a grin, releasing us into a fit of laughter.

I'm so glad Jesus sent His Holy Spirit to oil the cogs of my less-than-perfect memory. I need not worry about three months or one year from now. His Spirit will keep me on track, reminding me at just the right moments what I need to know.

Prayer Pathway: *Lord, please nudge my memory when my 'forgetter' works better than my 'rememberer'.*

God's Got My Number

Scripture Trail: Psalm 91:14-16, Isaiah 65:24, Jeremiah 33:3

Stepping Stone: Isaiah 65:24

> *"It shall come to pass that before they call, I will answer; and while they are still speaking, I will hear."*

God keeps His phone book up-to-date. He knows just exactly when I need a phone call, so I'll know He hasn't forgotten me.

Driving home from a doctor's appointment, I felt frustrated and discouraged. *Who me? Yes, definitely me.* A young friend came to mind who I wished I could talk with. Melodie had already maneuvered the medical road I had just begun to travel and I needed her advice.

Only problem was, I couldn't remember her new last name; she had recently married and I didn't have her phone number. But God knew she had my number and she just *happened* to call me that day to see if she had the correct mailing address for our home.

I can count on one finger how many times Melodie or I have chatted on the phone. Much of her time focuses on friendships with people of her own generation, as does mine. While loving each other, we circulate in two different worlds.

Less than five minutes after I arrived home, my phone rang with Melodie's call. When we finished our conversation, I felt as though I'd just experienced a person-to-person connection with heaven's hotline. She had no idea that she was God's angel, His messenger of love sent especially for me, when I most needed her.

After I hung up the phone, I imagined God writing giant letters across the sky, **"NORA ... THIS IS GOD ... I LOVE YOU!"**

Oh, please forgive me for running off. The phone's ringing.

Prayer Pathway: *What a relief that You know where to reach me, no matter how often I change my number.*

"Move, mountain ... move!"

Scripture Trail: Exodus 4:10-12, Matthew 17:20, Philippians 4:13

Stepping Stone: Exodus 4:12

> *"Now therefore, go, and I will be with your mouth and teach you what you shall say."*

Public speaking ranks number one on the list of experiences people fear most. Authorities on this subject say many people feel more afraid about speaking in front of a group than of facing death.

Naturally gregarious people find this phobia odd, if not amusing. We who battle hyperactive butterflies would like to put our butterfly net over their confident heads when they insist, "There's nothing to it! Just be yourself." If *myself* stands ridden with fear, what comfort is that statement supposed to give me?

Without a doubt, solo singing and public speaking are kissing cousins. To me, they are not just close cousins. They are twins. I will never forget the first solo I sang as a scared-to-my-toenails teenager. I felt light-headed and sick to my stomach. My knocking knees competed with my trembling voice for a special effects award. No one—including me—knew whether or not I would go through with singing that night.

The big moment, with all eyes focused on this paralyzed performer, came and went. Obviously, I lived to tell about it. The name of my solo selection proved so fitting: "Have Faith in God." *No kidding.* What's that scripture? "If you have the faith of a mustard seed ... you can tell a mountain to go jump in a lake." *(Peacock's Paraphrased Edition)* My faith was no bigger than the bottom of a ladybug's foot, but God made sure I survived my terrifying solo debut.

Faith in God moves mountains—even Mt. Fear.

Prayer Pathway: *Your Word says You are greater in me than my worst fears. You said it ... I believe it!*

154

"But God ..."

Scripture Trail: Exodus 4:10-12, Isaiah 50:4, Isaiah 57:15

Stepping Stone: Exodus 4:10

> *"Then Moses said to the LORD, '... I am not eloquent, neither before nor since You have spoken to Your servant; but I am slow of speech and slow of tongue.'"*

I like Moses. I identify with his insecurities. He questioned God. *Who am I to speak? Why would You use a tongue-tied person like me? What shall I say to these people?* Moses admitted he was flat-out scared.

Not unlike Moses, I come to God and complain about my fears and insecurities. Who am I to call myself a writer? God, you couldn't possibly use someone like me to influence others. Surely someone else could do a better job.

God speaks firmly to His unwilling children. He took Moses to the proverbial woodshed. When God the Father was done, He turned over part of Moses' responsibilities to his understudy, Aaron. God will get His work done, with or without me, but by refusing to be available, do I miss out on my *Promised Land* of blessing?

And so with my laundry list of insecurities, I'm asking God to use this wannabe writer. I ask that He would make up the difference in the skills I lack and touch readers who struggle with insecurity.

May I dare to believe God would use me, despite persistent anxiety when He calls me to a task? *But God, I can't do ... but God, who am I to ... but God, surely someone else would ...* my long list continues.

What would happen if I replace my 'But God ...' excuses with 'Yes, Lord, I will ...'? *Imagine that.* God would do what only God can do—in spite of me.

Prayer Pathway: *Lord, I ask for courage so that 'Yes, I will ...' may outnumber my 'But, God ...' response.*

Transformers

Scripture Trail: Ezra 9:6, Psalm 40:1-3, Psalm 143:8

Stepping Stone: Psalm 143:8

> *"Cause me to hear Your loving kindness in the morning, for in You do I trust; cause me to know the way in which I should walk."*

Parenting one last teenager revealed my shortcomings as a mother. I felt inadequate, despite already weathering 25 years of raising teens. This child's role in my discouragement reminded me of transformer toys—those plastic gizmos that change from cars into super heroes, from robots to spaceships, from houses to hamburgers. My teenager transformed into a mirror, complete with GPS signals aimed at me. On cue, this darling reflector revealed my failures.

After a lively "discussion" with my young charge ... well okay, I admit it ... after an emotion-charged argument I sat down for a pity party, complete with a box of tissues. While I later rested on the couch, I unwound enough to see my fault in our quarrel.

As I talked to God and told Him (and then later, my child) how sorry I was for losing it, I wondered: *God, are you sure I'm the person for this parenting job? After all these years, I still can't get it right.*

I jumped when the phone rang, interrupting my self-flagellation. A young woman called who I hadn't spoken to in twenty years. I had worked with during her high school years. We laughed over the challenges of our past student/adult relationship. She profusely thanked me for sticking with her through that turbulent season.

I hung up the phone, overwhelmed by her kind words. God knew how much I needed the encouragement she offered. From high school loafer to heaven's messenger—nice transformation, don't you think?

Prayer Pathway: *Transform my weakness into Your strength, as only You can do.*

Comfort Zone

Scripture Trail: Psalms 17:6-8, Psalm 56:3, Isaiah 26:3

Stepping Stone: Psalm 56:3

"Whenever I am afraid, I will trust in You."

My earliest memory of stepping outside my comfort zone came from sleeping with my grandmother. Grammy traveled from Texas to visit her kinfolk in Oregon. I had only met her once before when our family made a brief trip to Texas, so I didn't know her well.

My grandmother was a large lady—the perfect soft grandma size. I soon discovered her ample lap a wonderful place to cuddle. My memories are sketchy of Grammy's stay with us, other than bedtime.

For some reason, my parents designated me *the chosen one* to sleep with her. I wriggled into my pajamas. Ready for bed, I felt fine *until* … Grammy sat down beside me and proceeded to take out her teeth. I had never seen false teeth.

If that wasn't enough, she used an inhaler—another first-time sight for this young'un. On those memorable nights, I scarcely breathed as I slid under the covers next to my toothless, wheezing grandma.

Now, when I recall sleeping with Grammy, I chuckle. She didn't roll over and squish me. Her false teeth didn't jump out of their container and bite me. Thanks to the inhaler, she even kept breathing all night long … and wonder of wonders, so did I.

By stepping outside my comfort zone, free will or not, I now delight in the memories of sleeping with my grandmother. I wonder how many more priceless treasures God has in store for me, if only I will trust Him and face the unknown.

Prayer Pathway: *I can dare take risks, knowing that You, Father, have something good in store for me.*

Gone Fishin'

Scripture Trail: Psalm 4:8, Psalm 31:3, Psalm119:116-117

Stepping Stone: Psalm 119:117

> *"Hold me up, and I shall be safe, and I shall observe Your statutes continually."*

"Let's go fishing." Daddy's question easily held my attention. He had no problem getting me up before the rooster opened his beady eyes, belting out a cock-a-doodle-doo.

We went out on Lacamas Lake, not far from home. The waters gently rippled near the shore's edge. Before Dad untied the boat from the dock, he always made sure I wore my life jacket. My young mind questioned why he did this, when the lake seemed so calm and safe.

Along with us, lots of other fishermen threw their hooks in the water to catch *the big one*. Several boats larger than ours skimmed past us, while searching for the perfect fishing spot. The splashing wake rocked our small vessel. Had I stood without Daddy watching, I could have lost my balance, resulting in one careless kid overboard.

When Dad trolled near the shore, he cautiously navigated around limbs and rocks hidden under the water's surface. Bumping into just one obstruction could cause an unplanned dive into the lake. As a child, I was not strong enough, or skilled enough, to swim even a few yards to land. Water logged clothing would have quickly dragged me under.

As I think about those fishing trips, Jesus reminds me that He's my life preserver. Without Him, the wake of negative influences, life's hidden snares, and weighty cares of this world could sink me. As I face each day's challenges, He holds my head above the waters that threaten to drown me.

Prayer Pathway: *Dear Lord, thank You for Your life-saving instruction that preserves me from danger.*

Jesus, I give these fears to You:

_____

_____

_____

_____

_____

_____

_____

_____

_____

_____

_____

_____

_____

_____

_____

_____

I lay every burden and joy at the feet of Jesus.

"Faith
in God
moves mountains
—even
Mt. Fear."

At His Mercy

When life seems a desert, endless and cold
In the long night of suffering, to fall
Feeling hopeless while dark clouds unfold
Your gentle words bid me recall

I'm at His mercy and I never had it so good.

When dreams held long and close to my heart,
Promises no longer seem mine to embrace
The heavens like brass refusing to part
Your loving counsel reveals The Lord's grace

I'm at His mercy and I never had it so good.

When fears shadow my nights and my days
Hope eludes my searching, His peace to know
Tears blinding my eyes from The Son's rays
Your faith tested and tried, His glory does show

I'm at His mercy and I never had it so good.

In loving memory of my dear friend,
Linda Dunakin
I oft remember her words:
"I'm at His mercy
and I never had it so good!"

Daddy Walking

Steps

Agree With Me
Poem

*"Uphold my steps in Your paths,
that my footsteps may not falter."
Psalm 17:5*

Daddy Walking

Scripture Trail: John 5:19, John 17:20-21, 2 John 1:4

Stepping Stone: John 5:19

> *"Then Jesus answered and said to them, 'Most assuredly, I say to you, the Son can do nothing of Himself, but what He sees the Father do ...'"*

Back in the *when-I-was-a-kid* days, discarded coffee cans provided opportunities for great play times. After measuring twine to just the right length to hold in our hands, we farm kids strung it through holes punched in the tops of two cans. *Tah dah!* Instant stilts. Feeling a foot taller, we enjoyed countless hours clunking around on those tin cans.

When my children were little they clamored for another kind of fun that I called, "Daddy walking." Our kids stepped onto Arlen's size 13 feet and off Daddy and child went in tandem through the house. Giggles filled the air as they took giant-sized steps while riding along on Daddy's shoes. Falling off his feet didn't bother them. They just got right back on, and then off they went again with carefree joy. Nothing interrupted their laughter ... *until* a child had to give their turn to a brother or sister.

I often think about the special relationship Jesus has with His Father. I don't picture Jesus stepping on God's feet and the two of them walking off together, but He lived to follow in His Daddy God's footsteps. While their relationship surpasses feet-on-feet, Jesus bases His every move on what He sees His Father do.

The intimacy Jesus shares with His Father outshines even the closest earthly daddy/child relationship. God's son invites me to know His Abba like He does. There must be a scripture where Jesus says, "Your turn to Daddy walk with Abba Father. Go for it!"

Prayer Pathway: *Jesus, will You please show me how to follow in Daddy God's footsteps, just like You?*

Wordless Wonder

Scripture Trail: Genesis 1:10, Job 38:8-11, John 1:14

Stepping Stone: Job 38:8

> *"Or who shut in the sea with doors when it burst forth and issued from the womb ..."*

At 14 years of age, I walked over the crest of a sand dune and beheld the Pacific Ocean for the first time. I gasped at the vast sea that left me stunned and speechless. The endless expanse of water rolled in powerful waves that receded, only to repeat the cycle, but never in the same pattern twice. The beautiful horizon seemed infinitely far away, stretching farther than I could ever imagine.

Moments of first-time discovery become treasures that I tuck away in my memory bank where I retrieve them for the pure enjoyment they offer. Riding a bike for the first time on my own ... what a sense of freedom! High school graduation ... my spirit soared as I threw my tasseled cap in the air. Had someone wanted me to pose and recreate a snapshot of my delight ... well, can we say *impossible*?

And then came my wedding day when I said, "I do." The most eloquent recounting of the wedding guests' recollections could not recapture what I felt when I looked into my bridegroom's eyes.

How does a new parent describe the emotions, never before experienced at hearing their baby's first cry? What's it like to celebrate a fiftieth wedding anniversary? I don't know. I'm still waiting for that half-century milestone.

And some awesome day in the future, for the very first time, I will behold my Savior, face to face. As His majesty renders me speechless, He will understand the feelings I cannot express.

Prayer Pathway: *My King, I can hardly wait for that matchless moment when I see You for the very first time.*

Junk Collector

Scripture Trail: Isaiah 59:11-12, Jeremiah 30:17, John 6:37

Stepping Stone: John 6:37

> *"All that the Father gives Me will come to Me, and the one who comes to Me I will by no means cast out."*

"We buy and sell used cars." Signs posting these words usually mean what they say. So when I wrecked my car (by the way, the tree won) I looked up wrecking yards in the yellow pages. I remembered seeing ads inviting people to bring in their old cars, for which they would receive a modest payment. I figured all I needed to do was call and tell them my wreck was on its way.

Silly me. I thought wrecking yards bought wrecks. Three phone calls later … and only after the person from the third wrecking yard talked to his buyer, did he graciously agree to take my demolished car.

Maybe my asking price was too high: "You pick it up, it's yours." Parting out the engine alone would bring some decent bucks. The tires would give the buyer a profit, even after paying for towing. Scrap metal value was surely worth a few greenbacks.

Picky. Picky. Picky. That's how I saw the big-time power brokers who decided which wrecks merited their investment. From my point of view, *you've seen one wreck, you've seen 'em all. No big deal.*

On the other hand, I know The Buyer of wrecked lives Who throws out the word *picky*. The most battered life doesn't faze Him.

I don't have to go through some middleman to get God's confirming nod. He accepts me with only one condition: *I must call on Him.*

That's it—no rejection—acceptance for sure and certain.

Prayer Pathway: *Jesus, I marvel that no matter how wrecked my life, You want me—always.*

Elmer

Scripture Trail: Psalms 94:19, Isaiah 40:1, 1Thessalonians 5:11-13

Stepping Stone: 1 Thessalonians 5:11

> *"Therefore comfort each other and edify one another, just as you also are doing."*

His name was Elmer. So was my Dad's. With his thin frame and remaining fringes of gray hair, he even looked a little like Daddy.

Cantankerous. That word describes Elmer and my dad. They always had something to say, no matter the topic. Perhaps their longevity entitled them to know a little about everything. I didn't mind. The tales they spun intrigued me.

I met Elmer when I sang at Lambert House, the adult day care center he attended. We sang, laughed, and loved God together. He stole my heart when he gave me a silver dollar after I presented a program at the center. I still have the shiny token of his affection.

A couple of years went by and I became a Lambert House employee. My previous monthly trips helped me feel acquainted with the staff. Nevertheless, I still had first-day jitters about starting my new job.

I arrived at work that memorable morning, walked in the door, and there sat Elmer—front and center. From his wheelchair, he greeted me with a beaming smile and arms extended. I'd worked other places over the years, but never had I experienced such a warm welcome on my first day at a new job.

When I enter heaven's gates, neither Jesus nor Elmer will wait for me from a wheelchair. I also know that I want to hear Jesus' voice first. *Sorry, Elmer.* Regardless, I have a sneaking hunch they'll both greet me with arms open wide.

Prayer Pathway: *What a relief to know that I need not have any jitters my first day in heaven.*

When Plans Plop

Scripture Trail: Psalm 139:24, Psalm 143:10, James 4:13-15

Stepping Stone: Psalm 143:10

> *"Teach me to do Your will, for You are my God; Your Spirit is good. Lead me in the land of uprightness."*

I swung my feet over the edge of the bed and planted them on the floor. Time to start a new day.

I'm going to scrub the kitchen floor, including the hidden corners. Why stop there? The carpets could use a shampooing which means vacuuming first. While I'm at it, why not whip up Arlen's favorite banana pudding recipe? And I need to dust. Yes, it's going to be a productive day.

All right! Let me at the vacuum cleaner. Listen to that motor hum. Snap! Oh man, no time to buy a new belt. Okay. Let's try the kitchen floor. Don't tell me I forgot to buy floor cleaner and dusting spray yesterday. Three strikes. *Not good.*

I have one last chance to redeem myself. Banana pudding, here I come. What?! Who's the rascal that used up the eggs and didn't tell me?

Can I hit a rewind button and go back to when my feet touched the floor this morning? Is it possible God has different plans for my day? Perhaps I could visit a neighbor instead of scrubbing the kitchen floor and dusting. I can't vacuum the carpets with a broken-down machine. How about relaxing with a good book?

Now for the banana pudding ... I'd best keep that idea *my little secret,* lest I break my hubby's heart.

When the best plans for my day crumble, maybe it's time for me to learn to kick back and say, "It's okay, God. It's really okay."

Prayer Pathway: *God, I want to let You set the agenda for my day.*

Divine Appointments

Scripture Trail: Deuteronomy 26:8, Daniel 4:2-3, Acts 7:36

Stepping Stone: Daniel 4:2

> *"I thought it good to declare the signs and wonders that the Most High God has worked for me."*

Deer crossing signs stand sentinel along nearby farming roads. My daily routine often takes me past one of these yellow diamonds. Out driving one day, I wondered, *why does the, county, or whoever, bother to put up those signs? Deer never even come near them.*

Within seconds of my rambling thoughts, three deer trotted across the road from a nearby field. Cantering between my car and the sign, their graceful heads held high, they sent a clear message: "We know how to read. What's your problem?"

I happened along at the right place at the right moment to witness these animals obeying the warning sign. Alas! I didn't have a camera to prove it, but I felt as though I'd just experienced a divine appointment.

I recall other instances when I felt as though God showed up in the car and laughed with me. As I drove, I sang along with a CD that played lyrics by Bill Gaither: *"It's beginning to rain, says the voice of the Father."* At that moment, on cue, rain began splattering my windshield. I sensed God chuckling with me.

On another occasion, during a long road trip, I napped while Arlen drove. As we traveled the freeway at 60 mph, I opened my sleepy eyes and glanced over at the car alongside us. No driver! I jumped awake and soon realized the driverless vehicle was in-tow. No doubt, God laughed at my befuddled brain.

God's timing ... always perfect. Imagine that!

Prayer Pathway: Your divine appointments, significant or silly—God, I don't want to miss a single one!

Parental Job Posting

Scripture Trail: Psalm 127:3-5, Proverbs 22:6, Ephesians 6:4

Stepping Stone: Psalm 127:3

> *"Behold, children are a heritage from the LORD, the fruit of the womb is a reward."*

Employment: Social Services

POSITIONS AVAILABLE IMMEDIATELY. FT Parent 24/7. No days off. Below minimum wage. Bi-lingual. Valid driver's license preferable. On-the-job-training, regardless of prior experience. Advancement possible in 18 years. Retirement Plan: None. Health Plan: High risk coverage required. Vacation Time: Limited. Bonuses: Guaranteed with grandchildren. If interested, please call Jeremiah 33:3.

Who in their right mind would apply for this job posting? Every year, billions around the world land this too-good-to-be-true opportunity.

Babies seldom come accompanied by a parenting manual. The learning curve for new parents requires they hit the ground running. How quickly they discover that their bundle of joy demands their attention "every o'clock." *Sunrise...Sunset...*yep, this is *"the little girl I carried,"* and as far as *"the little boy at play ..."* he could take some lessons in letting mommy and daddy sleep.

"Advancement in 18 years?" Not likely. Junior and Sissy usually decide that the *exciting* independence they clamored for looks pretty scary. Why give up a nest with free rent?

Retirement? You've got to be kidding! Read the fine print buried discreetly on the back page of the employment contract:

"Once a parent ... always a parent."

Bi-lingual? Mama must become proficient at interpreting baby's babbling. Teen-speak? Well...forget translating their lingo. They operate under the mantra: "Keep Mom and Pop guessing."

No other vocation compares with parenting for challenging a person's limits. No other calling gives greater job satisfaction. As for the bonuses: If you don't have a grandchild, borrow one!

Prayer Pathway: *No matter my role in a child's life, help me fulfill my sacred responsibility to Your youngsters.*

Fostered Love

Scripture Trail: Deuteronomy 31:6, Joshua 1:7-8, 1 Samuel 17:37

Stepping Stone: 1 Samuel 17:37

> *"Moreover David said, 'The LORD, who delivered me from the paw of the lion and from the paw of the bear, He will deliver me from the hand of this Philistine …'"*

Superheroes. They leap tall buildings in a single bound, take down giants that cause grown men to tremble in fear, and single handedly turn the tide of battles.

I personally know some superheroes. Many of them, very young, but rough around the edges, came to live in the Peacock home. They've run the gauntlet of bureaucracies and lived to tell about it. They've fought their battles, while cut off from everything and everyone familiar. Many have slain the giant of worthlessness to become well-adjusted adults.

These intrepid dragon slayers wear a label that puts them on the defensive. Foster children quickly learn to conceal the title branded on their chest, lest the questions begin: "Why are you in foster care? Where are you parents? Why don't you act like other kids?" Spoken or unspoken, the thoughtless barbs hit their mark.

I've discovered a secret about these children that numerous moves between foster homes can't squelch. Multiple changes in caseworkers can't bury this mystery in *the system*. In spite of the infamous label, these kids grow up and turn their pain into passion for the downtrodden. They bravely break the cycle of dysfunction in their lives to become *adoring* and *adored* parents. They find their God-given value and, in return, they impart hope to the hopeless.

To my foster children, all now grown, you have fought the good fight, with heroic courage in the face of great pain. I've watched you overcome. You have taught me much—I am forever grateful.

Prayer Pathway: *Father, please bless every precious foster child and help them know how much You love them.*

Milestones

Scripture Trail: Psalm 143:10, Proverbs 23:24-25, Galatians 4:18

Stepping Stone: Proverbs 23:25

> *"Let your father and your mother be glad, and let her who bore you rejoice."*

Kenlee takes her first steps, falls down on her padded bottom, and the room full of parents, grandparents, aunts and uncles, erupts with glee. The little darling looks around at all the attention, brushing off the fact that her first foray into this adventure called *walking* was so short-lived.

Lauren holds out her small hand, proudly displaying another baby tooth that has come out. Her eyes sparkle with anticipation at the dollar bill that she knows will 'magically' appear under her pillow the next morning. Tooth fairy wages have gone up! Teasing about this mythical being elicits giggles and a melt-your-heart toothless grin.

Joshie and Jo Jo get their driver's license and they endure the requisite ribbing: "Here he comes, clear the decks … warn me before you take off … are the airbags working?" The teenagers shrug off the ribbing and grin as they show off the 2 x 3 cards. They couldn't care less whether or not their mug shots look cool.

Wedding bells peal, and mom and dad swipe away tears as the bride and groom run the gauntlet of rice raining down. Horns honk and clattering tin cans fade into the distance as tired parents walk back into the church holding hands, not trusting their voices to work. Just yesterday was filled with baby steps, baby teeth, and car keys.

Mom and Dad trade in children's baby books, school pictures, and wedding albums for Grandma's and Grandpa's brag books.

Milestones leave precious memories … Lord, may they linger.

Prayer Pathway: *Jesus, with every milestone in my life, You cheer me on. You're The Best!*

Pomp and Circumstance

Scripture Trail: Psalm 127:3, Proverbs 22:6, 2 Timothy 1:3-5

Stepping Stone: Proverbs 22:6

> *"Train up a child in the way he should go, and when he is old he will not depart from it."*

All across our nation, accompanied by the strains of *Pomp and Circumstance,* young people walk across a stage to receive a long-awaited piece of paper. With hard-earned diplomas in hand, they march forward, one step closer to accomplishing their dreams.

At the end of a long evening of speeches, choral songs, receiving diplomas, and the requisite student pranks, the long-awaited moment arrives when seniors move their tassels from one side of their cap to the other, sealing their graduate status. Joyous shouts erupt as students toss their mortarboards high into the air. Confetti flies, balloons float skyward.

While students celebrate, moms, dads and grandparents experience a myriad of emotions. Some breathe deep sighs of relief while others weep happy tears. Many relatives and friends relive their own graduation. They know life will never be the same for their special student—high school days now a thing of the past.

When I wait in the bleachers to root for my graduate, I enjoy watching parents and grandparents arriving. Some stop to catch their breath every few steps. Others walk with canes, every stair step a struggle. Many older adults come in spite of obvious physical pain. They cherish their VIP.

Graduates, speaking from podiums, often express thanks for their parents' sacrificial love and support. Some students even mention friends and other relatives. Whatever the relationship to the teen in cap and gown, I can play an important part in their life. They need me. What a privilege.

Prayer Pathway: *Lord, may I make a difference in a child's future.*

Coming Home

Scripture Trail: Luke 15:6, Luke 15:21-24, Hebrews 8:12

Stepping Stone: Luke 15:6

> *"And when he comes home, he calls together his friends and neighbors, saying to them, 'Rejoice with me, for I have found my sheep which was lost!"*

He walked in the church door likely wondering how people would react. Years of drug addiction had taken its toll. His face looked haggard, but his eyes said, "I've found my way back home." He'd returned to his Savior and to his church family.

Person after person walked over to Ross and embraced him that Sunday morning. From the pulpit, our pastor added his greeting, "Welcome home, brother. We're glad you're here."

"Amens" and "Hallelujahs" echoed in the sanctuary.

While our rejoicing continued, the real work began. Our brother needed more than a warm slap on the back and a hug around the neck. From years of drug abuse, he'd lost much—his health, his family, and the ministry in which he'd been so effective. He faced a difficult road ahead.

God isn't finished with Ross. His heavenly Father proclaims, "My son's back! Kill the fatted calf. It's party time!"

While God dances in celebration over His son, He also rolls up His holy sleeves for the work to come. For the lonely nights ahead when tears fall for the family Ross has lost, God says, "I'm here, Son." When his body screams for just one more fix, God promises, "I will be your strength." When Ross weeps bitter tears of regret for those he's hurt, when he would give anything to undo the past, God says, "I have forgiven your sins and remember them no more."

Such tender love, such amazing grace … how sweet the sound.

Prayer Pathway: God, *may I serve as an instrument in* Your hands *to bring restoration and healing.*

Just like Jesus, I want to walk in my Father's footsteps. For me that looks like:

_____

_____

_____

_____

_____

_____

_____

_____

_____

_____

_____

_____

_____

_____

I lay every burden and joy at the feet of Jesus.

"On the
other hand,
I know The Buyer
of wrecked lives
whose heart defies
the word
picky."

Agree With Me

Dear God, I called to You in the hours of the night
You sent a friend my way to make my burden light
When on the phone, in the darkness not alone
My friend said these words, "Agree with me."

    Agree with me, from you pain you'll be set free
    Agree with me, and know His victory
    Agree with me, in Jesus peace you'll truly be
    Agree now in prayer, agree with me

My friend, I come to you in Jesus' precious name
This peace He gives to me, He'll give to you the same
Now give to Him the cry of your heart
To you, His peace He will impart

    Agree with me, from you pain you'll be set free
    Agree with me, and know His victory
    Agree with me, in Jesus peace you'll truly be
    Agree now in prayer, agree with me

Written in loving memory of
my spiritual dad, Dean Park.
In a time of great pain, he spoke words
of life, assurance, and hope for the future.

A Child's Heart

Steps

"I balanced!"

"Let it snow! Let it snow!"

Bragging Rights

"Wow is me!"

Solomon's Understudy

Thundering Turtles

"Why?"

Deck the Halls

Homespun

Hope for Tomorrow

Moving On

To the Feet of The King
Poem

"Therefore, whoever humbles himself
as this little child is the greatest
in the kingdom of heaven." Matthew 18:4

"I balanced!"

Scripture Trail: 2 Kings 12:15, Job 31:6, Ezekiel 45:9-10

Stepping Stone: 2 Kings 12:15

> *"Moreover they did not require an account from the men into whose hand they delivered the money to be paid to workmen, for they dealt faithfully."*

People who work in banks handle lots of money. My family and friends enjoyed teasing me when I became a vault teller. "Can't you bring me home just one eensy-weensy stack of hundreds?"

Part of each day, my boss let me escape the vault to work a teller window. Customer contact always beat counting dirty bills. In one memorable incident, a woman came to another teller's window. She had a check to cash for 50 cents. Checks for under a dollar weren't uncommon, but this one was special ... *so special* that Bugs Bunny himself signed it.

The Bugs Bunny saga only got better. Our astute teller actually cashed the check. This red-faced employee endured far more than 50 cents worth of ribbing from his ornery coworkers.

Bugs Bunny bandits aside, the tellers had to balance their drawer right after closing. About ten minutes into counting, happy exclamations of, "I balanced!" filtered down the teller row. A few groans and several recounts also figured in the mix.

"I balanced!" and "Oh, no!" entered my vocabulary as well.

At the end of each workday, little ears waited for Mommy to get home. My kindergarten son, Jimmy, came bouncing in the door after school one afternoon announcing to the world, "I balanced!" Clueless to the banking aspect of his proclamation, he knew those two words meant happiness for Mama.

Should I see a big smile on Jesus' face when I finish my life's work, I'll know I finally balanced!

Prayer Pathway: *Lord, how I long to hear You say, "Well done, good and faithful servant ... you balanced!"*

"Let it snow! Let it snow!"

Scripture Trail: Job 37:5-7, Proverbs 25:13, Isaiah 1:18

Stepping Stone: Job 37:6

> *"For He says to the snow, 'Fall on the earth'; likewise to the gentle rain and the heavy rain of His strength."*

I love *Aha!* moments. How glad I am that God knows how to get past my stick-in-the-mud tendencies.

As a young mother, I enjoyed late evenings with a good book whenever I could. One night, well after bedtime for my kiddos, my oldest munchkin's tousled head peeked around the corner. My automatic mother's reaction kicked into gear. *What are you doing up at this hour?*

I'd been soaking up a great novel, a story centered on God's grace. Just as I started to ask my grade school child what I thought a most logical and reasonable question, God reminded me, *Nora, it's snowing. Get a clue.*

My hopeful cherub asked, "Mama, can I play in the snow?" Thankfully, my lightning quick mind connected the weather with Eddy's late night appearance.

I paused from reading about God's mercy to see my little boy walk to the living room window and press his nose against the glass. And then the *Aha!* hit me. Snow means no school … which means freedom … and snow forts … which means snowball fights and building a snowman … and hot chocolate … and all kinds of fun!

Grace means no penalty for my sin … which means freedom … which means not trying to save myself by my works … which means God really loves me!

My son couldn't make snow anymore than I can create God's grace. Were I a young mom again, I'd huck the clock and ask my child, "Snowball fight, Kiddo?"

Prayer Pathway: *How I need Your loving grace, Jesus, that washes me whiter than snow.*

Bragging Rights

Scripture Trail: Matthew 19:13-14, Luke 18:16, 2 Timothy 1:5

Stepping Stone: 2 Timothy 1:5

> *"when I call to remembrance the genuine faith that is in you, which dwelt first in your grandmother Lois ... and I am persuaded is in you also."*

"*My grandpa* let me sit on his lap and drive the tractor!"

"Well, *my grandma* said I make the best chocolate chip cookies in the whole world!"

"That's nothing. *My grandma* takes her teeth out!"

My friends looked at me like ... *so what?! Lots of old people have false teeth.* But I had precious little ammunition to match their *can-you-top-this* grandpa and grandma stories. Raised apart from my grandparents, I had few memories of them. The teeth story was the best I could offer.

So what's a little girl to do? Years passed and my need for a grandparent in my life remained. At the ripe old age of 16, I went to work at a nursing home and soon realized *Cool beans! I've found them!*

Just take a gander at *my grandparent tales.* Grandma Ingrid knew the Von Trapp Family Singers, who inspired the movie, *The Sound of Music.* Another one of my unofficial grandmas hosted Mother Teresa in her home. And then Grandpa Horace was a three-star general, and Grandpa Otis descended from ... need I say more?

Now at age 63 and a grandma several times over, I recall that grandparent-sized void of my childhood. Compared to a generation ago, fewer seniors now live with—or even near—their adult children and grandchildren. I suspect that a lot of God's youngsters yearn for their own grandparent bragging rights. When they go looking, dare I raise my hand and say, "Pick me! Pick me!"

Prayer Pathway: *Please use me to fill the grandparent-sized need in the lives of Your little ones.*

"Wow is me!"

Scripture Trail: Psalm 121:5-8, Isaiah 49:10, Revelation 7:16

Stepping Stone: Isaiah 49:10

> *"They shall neither hunger nor thirst, neither heat nor sun shall strike them; for He who has mercy on them will lead them ..."*

From my place at the cash register, I watched a towheaded boy wander around the store checking out books, toys, and kid stuff. A hundred choices loomed before this two-foot tall charmer. He finally settled on a storybook about David and Goliath. Without a slingshot, my pint-sized customer conquered the giant named *Indecision.*

Daddy joined his son who clutched the all-important purchase in a chubby hand at the front counter. Dad informed me that the book was for their trip to Seattle. I looked down at Mr. Cuteness and said, "This is a hot day. When you get to Seattle, are you going to play in the water?"

With some effort, he looked over the counter's edge enough for his sparkling eyes to meet mine. Then up came his small hand, with three stubby fingers held high ... *well, sort of high.* "It's three hots!"

A boring adult might have settled for the over-used cliché, "It's so hot you could fry an egg on the sidewalk." But this little guy clearly knew what he meant.

I'm one to whine and complain big time when the mercury hits 90. I'm a total goner at 100 degrees. Thanks to my pint-sized customer's enthusiasm, I learned to view the heat with less groan and more "Wow!"

Children. God's wondrous creation sent for old fogies like me who need to see *Wow!* in every new day. Just maybe I'll not let the next heat wave make me so hot under the collar.

Prayer Pathway: *Even when life gets uncomfortable, help me to say "Wow!" instead of "Woe."*

Solomon's Understudy

Scripture Trail: Proverbs 20:15, Psalm 25:4-5, Proverbs 23:12

Stepping Stone: Proverbs 23:12

> *"Apply your heart to instruction, and your ears to words of knowledge."*

Now a high school graduate, Shali has always defined the word, precocious. This home-schooled child kept her mother, Ginny, scrounging for adequate teaching resources. As a six-year-old, Shali one day announced, "I want to become a info-ologist." Her Mama and I weren't quite sure we had heard her right, but Shali knew exactly what she said.

With considerable frustration and several repetitions of her statement, Ginny's young scholar tried another tack. With an exasperated sigh she restated her point. "You know ... biologist ... zoologist ... info-ologist!" By this time Shali wondered if she would have to spell out her statement for her less-than-astute mother and honorary auntie.

Ginny and I felt like saying, "Oh, now we get it!" even though we still weren't sure what Shali really meant. After further discussion with her, we decided Shali wanted to know ALL she could about EVERYTHING! Her appropriate use of the words *biologist* and *zoologist* left us wondering if she might not also pull off her academic goal. Forget the usual, "I want to be a nurse or a teacher," that so many little girls grab onto. She would become an Information Expert, i.e. an info-ologist.

The future holds bright promise for Shali. She will one day likely attain a Doctorate of Info-ology. When this day comes, her proud mother and elderly auntie will wait in the wings to seek her wise counsel.

I wonder if Solomon had a shingle hanging outside his door: "The Info-ologist is in."

Prayer Pathway: *When it comes to knowing you, Father, I want to become an info-ologist, just like Shali.*

Thundering Turtles?

Scripture Trail: Isaiah, 28:23, John 10:27, 1 Corinthians 13:9-11

Stepping Stone: 1 Corinthians 13:11

> *"When I was a child, I spoke as a child, I understood as a child, I thought as a child; but when I became a man, I put away childish things."*

Children excel at reinventing word meanings. Songs from church hymnals provide abundant opportunities for confusion. As a child, Arlen misunderstood "Bringing in the Sheaves." Surely he must have wondered why all the adults around him sang about "ringing in the sheets." Clothes were washed in ringer washers, so he connected this odd song with his mama's washing machine.

My Texas mother knew all about the dangers of snapping turtles that frequented the streams near her childhood home. Her parents warned her that if one of these critters chomped down on her hand, it wouldn't let go until 'it' thundered. *Thunder ... weather.* Seems clear, right? Mom later passed down the snapping turtle story to me, her little girl. I pictured one of the snapping buggers biting down on my hand and not letting go until the poor little thing shook itself silly, thus forcing open its chompers. The senseless animal would then fall to the ground.

True to children's thinking, my kiddos came up with a unique response to one of my own not-so-clear parental questions. When giving them a choice of cereal for breakfast I'd ask, "What *kind* do you want?" It wasn't long before a cutie pie informed me, "I want some *kind.*"

How often do I misconstrue my Daddy God's words? When He says, "Surrender!" is He talking about a showdown at the *OK Corral?* Or just maybe He means sweet surrender to His will. *Hmm ... sweet surrender ... sounds mighty good to me!*

Prayer Pathway: *Father, reveal to me any misunderstandings I have when You speak to me.*

"Why?"

Scripture Trail: Numbers 32:23, Job 31:6, Psalm19:13-14

Stepping Stone: Job 31:6

> *"Let me be weighed on honest scales, that God may know my integrity."*

Why does an ostrich stick its head in the sand? Why do possums hang by their tails, while skunks do what skunks do? Why do crabs walk sideways and flamingos stand on one leg? Why do tadpoles lose their tails and become frogs, while earthbound caterpillars transform into monarch butterflies that soar through the heavens?

Young children love to ask, "Why?" They see an obviously pregnant woman and ask, "Why is her tummy so big?" They see a man in a wheelchair and blurt out, "Why can't he walk?" Their inquisitive little minds don't worry about embarrassing someone. They just want a simple answer to a simple one-word question, "Why?" So what's the problem with that?

I'll never forget a story a minister told that scored a 10 on the Richter scale about a precocious child who asked, "Why?" How Mommy and Daddy ever rescued themselves from the moment, I have no idea.

A visiting preacher stayed with a family in the church while he conducted a week of special meetings. His first morning at the breakfast table, the father of the family asked the blessing over the plates of bacon, eggs, and biscuits. Young Amy piped up with, "Why did you pray, Daddy? We never pray at breakfast!" *Oh, to be a mouse in that preacher's pocket!*

Why? There's so much power in that three-letter word. When a child holds my life under the magnifying glass of their naïve innocence, will I burn or learn?

Prayer Pathway: *God, may I never burn with shame when I answer the question, "Why?"*

Deck the Halls

Scripture Trail: Psalm 89:15-16, Psalm 96:1, Isaiah 35:10

Stepping Stone: Psalm 96:1

> *"Oh, sing to the LORD a new song! Sing to the LORD, all the earth."*

Her eyes twinkled as she passed me in the hospital hallway. The white-haired Christmas caroler nodded and smiled while she continued singing. *The First Noel*, *Away in the Manger*, *Silent Night*, among many other familiar Yuletide songs, decked the halls as this Christmas angel strolled from room to room.

While I camped out beside my mother-in-law's hospital bed during Christmas week, I learned to listen for the elderly woman's sweet voice that trembled with age. I seldom had long to wait when she made her daily rounds. Making her circuit past one room after the other, she stepped inside Mom's door, each time stopping to sing glad tidings of the birth of her Savior.

With the ending of each song, she glanced down at the paper she held in her hand just long enough to recall the words for her next selection. Then off she went on her mission to share joy with another hurting patient spending their Christmas in the hospital.

This Christmas angel wasn't dressed in white flowing robes with wings and a halo. Instead, she walked the halls, dressed in a hospital gown and slippers. She left her hospital bed to tenderly impart sweet angel song.

Sickness faded in the gentle presence of God's Spirit that blanketed patients and families with comfort and hope. I'm convinced that the heavenly host is already having serious discussions about who gets to stand next to one singing saint when she someday joins their glorious heavenly choir.

Prayer Pathway: *In the midst of suffering, help me look past my pain and spread joy.*

Homespun

Scripture Trail: Isaiah 11:6, Daniel 10:10-12, Matthew 5:8

Stepping Stone: Isaiah 11:6

> *"The wolf also shall dwell with the lamb, the leopard shall lie down with the young goat, the calf and the young lion ... and a little child shall lead them."*

Church productions performed by homegrown stars offer priceless memories. After years of involvement in these grand galas of risk taking, I've seen some unforgettable moments.

In an Easter cantata, a choir member standing next to me had an attack of stage fright. As I sang a solo part, before my voice hit *b flat*, Karina passed out on the floor. The performer's mantra: "The show must go on," flashed through my mind, so I continued singing, while others carried the poor girl off stage. Surely, no one thought the impromptu activity belonged in the script.

One of my sons, as an infant, carried the role of baby Jesus in a Christmas program. Of course, Cory stole the show with his talent! An adult stood offstage, ready to fake a baby's cry. Wouldn't you know it? My little celebrity cried right on cue. He totally upstaged the adult understudy waiting in the wings.

In one country church play, live animals appeared in the Christmas stable scene. A child led an innocent goat across the stage, signs hanging over both sides of the animal's back. Guiding the goat *stage left,* the audience saw the word, LAMB. Leading the animal *stage right*, everyone saw the word, COW. Chuckles rippled through the congregation, while the little cast members beamed.

No one seems immune from rooting for nervous children or adults who forget their lines. The best part happens when the one-of-a-kind productions end.

No matter the mistakes, "Good job!" echoes all around.

Prayer Pathway: *Father, how precious that even in my homespun efforts to honor You—You exclaim, "Good job!"*

Hope for Tomorrow

Scripture Trail: Genesis 18:17-19, Proverbs 22:6, 1 Timothy 4:12

Stepping Stone: 1 Timothy 4:12

> *"Let no one despise your youth, but be an example to the believers in word, in conduct, in love, in spirit, in faith in purity."*

I own an irreplaceable book. Sunday school children in my church spent weeks illustrating a study they'd done in class. Finger painted animals, sequined grass, cotton ball clouds, and joyful angels fill the pages. A 3-D bird's nest perches on the front cover. Two young sisters, Melissa and Chelsea, brought the book to me at home. They also held my hands and prayed for me, not because they *had* to, but because they *wanted* to.

While I recovered from lymphoma, my grandsons Joshie and Jo Jo pitched in doing dishes, swept and mopped floors, and helped with whatever else Grandma needed. Their thoughtfulness made a most difficult time much easier.

Megan, now a young woman, completed two years of Job Corps training. Since meeting her at junior high age, I've had the privilege of being a big sister to her. I couldn't guess how many times she has called me expressing her concern for victims of whatever disaster.

Eric's kindness draws children like a magnet. The youngsters in our family plan weeks ahead for his next appearance at holiday gatherings. They follow their teenage cousin from the minute he arrives, knowing Eric will sit and hang out with them.

I've been told the following words were found on the ruins of a Roman wall: *"Young people are going to the dogs."* How wrong then— and how wrong to think so now. Our future shines bright. Just look at each of these amazing youngsters and convince me otherwise. Not a chance!

Prayer Pathway: *Father, show me ways to encourage children so that they feel appreciated and loved.*

Moving On

Scripture Trail: Isaiah 42:9, Philippians 3:13-14, Revelation 21:4

Stepping Stone: Revelation 21:4

> *"And God will wipe away every tear from their eyes; there shall be no more death, nor sorrow, nor crying. There shall be no more pain ..."*

The newspaper waits in the box, taunting me. I remove the paper, knowing it no longer belongs here, nor do I. So many memories merge one into another, waltzing in a melancholy dance.

A blue jay regales me with his song. Nestled in a tree, his triumphant tune pierces my heart. Clothed in royal blue, his extravagant vestments stand out against the barren winter branches. He offers his song to a brilliant blue sky, heedless that the heavens rival his own splendor.

An open field spreads its coarse blanket before me. Dreams remain buried in its untilled soil. Deer gently nibble at grassy stubble in the unfenced pasture, bringing quiet joy to my soul.

I close my eyes in sweet sadness. Children's and grandchildren's laughter echoes in my mind. How often their happy voices rippled to the heavens, while playing in the crisp country air.

And now I must move on. My thoughts will revisit this sanctuary of memories. I leave with deep gratitude for these years filled with pleasure and even pain. In pleasure I have reveled. In pain I have grown.

Young ones will laugh again, to a new tune in another place. The deer I enjoyed stroll away, deferring to scampering squirrels who, like me, find a new home. Birds will wing their way between the old and the new, touching my spirit like the wings of a dove.

Parting with the past, moving on to what the future holds, Father, You are there.

Prayer Pathway: *Holy Spirit, I am so grateful that Your sweet presence surrounds me wherever I go.*

Daddy God, I need You to kiss this 'owie' and make it all better:

_____

_____

_____

_____

_____

_____

_____

_____

_____

_____

_____

_____

_____

_____

_____

I lay every burden and joy at the feet of Jesus.

To the Feet of The King

The boy with his basket, to Jesus did bring
  His bread and his fish, to the feet of The King
   His heart swelled in awe as his offering so small
    Met the needs of the thousands, to the wonder of all

The widow's last coin, to Jesus did bring
  Her lack and her need, to the feet of The King
   Her heart swelled in awe as her offering so small
    Caused the praise of her Lord, to the wonder of all

A family so humble, to Jesus still brings
  Their love and their service, to the feet of The King
   Our hearts swell in wonder as your offering once small
    Has blessed beyond measure, to the wonder of all

"His lord said to him,
'Well done, good and faithful servant;
you have been faithful over a few things,
I will make you ruler over many things …'"
Matthew 23:23

Dedicated to Dennis & Charlotte Bischof,
founders of *Stop Hunger and Poverty Now.*
Your selfless labor reflects what it
means to follow in the footsteps of Jesus.

Walking with Jesus

P. Gates

Sacred Sandals

Scripture Trail: Exodus 3:4-5, Luke 7:44, Acts 7:33

Stepping Stone: Acts 7:33

> *"Then the LORD said to him, 'Take your sandals off your feet, for the place where you stand is holy ground."*

When did Jesus wear His first pair of sandals? Did He wiggle His tiny toes, puzzled over the scratchy things on His toddler feet? Did Mary chuckle when her son tripped while adjusting to the strange contraptions?

Jesus must have kicked off His sandals when He went fishing with his friends on riverbanks. How many hot afternoons did He sink His toes into the squishy cool mud? Maybe He challenged the neighborhood boys to a foot race, coming back for His sandals after He'd left the other guys in the dust.

Jesus' sandals carried Him to the well where the Samaritan woman received His gift of grace and hope. He walked the paths fishermen trekked, calling them to leave everything and follow Him.

Jesus' sandaled feet entered rooms where death hovered near. He stood close by and spoke life to hearts held hostage to hopelessness. One moment He moved with tender steps. The next, He stormed into the temple, displacing greed with reverence.

Did Jesus' sandals rip when He stumbled under the weight of the cross? Did someone pick up His blood-spattered sandals after the soldiers nailed His precious feet to the cross? Did that person, whose hands clutched those dusty sandals, gaze at the leather straps and remember the cat of nine tails? Did he tremble in holy awe?

Sandals clad the feet of my King, who clothed me in His mercy and forgiveness. In heartfelt wonder, I remove my shoes, for I am standing on holy ground.

Prayer Pathway: *Thank You, my dear Savior, for walking the painful road to Calvary, so that I may dance the streets of gold.*

More than anything, Jesus, I want You to know:

_____

_____

_____

_____

_____

_____

_____

_____

_____

_____

_____

_____

_____

_____

_____

I lay every burden and joy at the feet of Jesus.

"He
stood close by
and spoke life
to hearts
held hostage to
hopelessness."

Sandals

In sandals Christ made His way to the cross
Bearing my shame, to suffer such loss
Worn sandals on feet so holy, so pure
Forging a pathway, so narrow—yet sure

Sandals worn humbly on the feet of my King
Such selfless love makes my heart long to sing
Of glory that only The Savior should know
Yet on His children He chose to bestow

In sandals He held me close to His heart
As He trod dusty roads, His love to impart
Leaving the joy of His Father's embrace
Those sandals brought unspeakable grace

May I never forget the price Jesus paid
In sandals kneeling for me as He prayed
His sandals removed, He died all alone
In exchange for His crown—my sin to atone

"If anyone serves Me,
let him follow Me,
and where I am,
there My servant will be also,
If anyone serves Me,
him My Father will honor."
John 12:26